T0369009

THROUGH THE VALLEY

RICHARD AND ROBIN JOHNSON

WESTBOW
PRESS
A DIVISION OF THOMAS NELSON

Scriptures taken from the Holy Bible, New International Version®,
NIV®. Copyright © 1973, 1978, 1984, 2011 by Biblica, Inc.™ Used by
permission of Zondervan. All rights reserved worldwide. www.zondervan.com
The "NIV" and "New International Version" are trademarks registered
in the United States Patent and Trademark Office by Biblica, Inc.™

WestBow Press books may be ordered through booksellers or by contacting:

WestBow Press
A Division of Thomas Nelson
1663 Liberty Drive
Bloomington, IN 47403
www.westbowpress.com
1-(866) 928-1240

Cover photo by: Heather Cherie' Photography
Cover Design by: Madi Walker

ISBN: 978-1-4497-9796-6 (sc)
ISBN: 978-1-4497-9797-3 (hc)
ISBN: 978-1-4497-9795-9 (e)

Library of Congress Control Number: 2013910614

Printed in the United States of America.

WestBow Press rev. date: 6/14/2013

TABLE OF CONTENTS

Introduction xiii

Chapter 1   The Valley Begins 1

Chapter 2   The Unknown Valley 6

Chapter 3   Growing Deeper 15

Chapter 4   Deeper Still...24

Chapter 5   A True Lesson In Trust 33

Chapter 6   A Valley Of Three 43

Chapter 7   Between The Rock and Hard Place 52

Chapter 8   A Miracle In The Making.............................. 59

Chapter 9   Our Ever-Present Help In Cleveland.............. 69

Chapter 10   The Beautiful Body 79

Chapter 11   More Hurdles In The Valley 84

Chapter 12   2011…The Year For Change 97

Chapter 13   From The Colorado Valley to the
             Missouri Valley 107

Chapter 14   The Valley of the Shadow of Death................ 120

Chapter 15   Peace In The Midst of the Storm 125

Chapter 16   When Health Fails In Marriage 131

DEDICATION

To Our Lord Jesus:

The valley has been long and arduous at times, but we know we cannot do it on our own. You have led us, helped us, and provided for us in the most difficult of times. Thank you, Lord! We dedicate this work and our lives to you. You are faithful to the end.

To Our Children and Grandchildren:

You have walked this journey with us and have also walked through the valley. You have unselfishly given of yourselves while watching sometimes from afar. We love you and desire all of you to leave godly legacies that will endure for eternity.

ACKNOWLEDGMENTS

We would like to acknowledge and thank the following people for their extraordinary contribution(s) to our book and lives in helping to make "Through the Valley" a reality for us:

Mr. Tom Young in Ozark, Missouri: Your editing skills and talents, for which we never would have been able to adequately portray our journey in a professional manner. You are a God-given blessing.

Mr. Matthew Smith in Springfield, Missouri: His quick and skilled editing and formatting gifts, which have expedited the publishing process for us. You have been a blessing, Sir.

Miss Madi Walker in Ozark, Missouri: Her graphic skills in the design of our awesome cover design. You are a blessing to us, Madi.

Heather Amer of Heather Cherie' Photography in Springfield, Missouri: You have captured our lives in these past five years in pictures, and the memories you have given us are priceless. Your contribution to our author picture on the front and back covers will remain with our legacy. We love you.

Pastors John and Debbie Lindell, Lead Pastors James River Assembly in Ozark, Missouri: Coming back to Missouri was not as difficult for us in knowing the church we would return to was under your unwavering and integral leadership. You have fed us each Sunday and continue to lead and serve in ways that exemplifies true Christ followers. Thank you for your leadership and prayers during our long, physical trials. You are a great blessing to us and so many.

Our former congregation of First Assembly of God and the La Junta, Colorado community: You stood with us and prayed for us through some of the most difficult times of our physical and spiritual lives while we served there in that great southeast Colorado town. It was our honor to serve you and love you as Christ does, and we will forever be indebted to you for the love you showed us while serving you in the midst of some very difficult days.

The many pastors and colleagues in the Rocky Mountain District Council of the Assemblies of God: Your prayers, support and love will always remain a source of strength and encouragement to us, and specifically to our former presbyter and friends Darryl and Debbie Johnson of Fowler, Colorado— your incredible friendship and love to us was irreplaceable while we were in the thick of the spiritual and physical battles. Only eternity will be able to reveal how your Jonathan and David relationship with us helped us to go on another day. We are eternally grateful for your family and friendship.

Our many, many friends throughout the United States who have held us up in prayer and support while we've walked "Through the Valley." We could never have survived or endured this race without you. We value your prayers and treasure your friendship. We know we've been able to continue on this journey because you have lifted our names before the Lord. We love you.

The many donors who contributed to the successful publishing of our story and journey, *Through the Valley*. It is our vision and hope that our journey will go on and inspire and encourage many others who come after us to look to the One who has led us. Those of you who have contributed financially have also contributed to the countless lives who will now be changed by putting their trust in Him who makes every valley low and crooked path straight. God bless you.

INTRODUCTION

Valley experiences are all relevant and unique. As human beings, we struggle with many different issues in this life, but every valley we walk through can and should be a learning and growing experience for us. Some walk through deep valleys while others seemingly go through a lesser degree of valley experiences. One thing is certain: We all go through difficult times, but how we deal with them makes the difference in the outcome. As I look back on my own life, I can see many difficult experiences that only serve to remind me of unique situations in each case. Did I emerge from each of those experiences a victor and a ten-foot spiritual giant? No. Every time was a learning experience for me, and I had the opportunity to grow from them or become embittered by my own selfish desires for a better outcome.

As I look at the scriptural examples of dealing with difficult times, I'm reminded of many biblical characters that went through some of the worst situations life can bring. We must remember that they did not know their outcome. We have the great privilege of reading their outcome before the story begins. These characters were people just like you and me who had to deal with different degrees of life's difficult situations. The Bible and the stories of truth contained within its timeless pages bring hope and encouragement to my heart. The stories of men and women who went through those difficulties so long ago are meant to help us understand and grow from their valley experiences.

One of my favorite biblical stories is Job. While none of us would ever trade places with Job in his ongoing trials, he serves to remind us that Godly men go through difficult times and can be victorious. In case you don't know the story, allow me to recap the highlights of a circumstance that would push most over the edge. Job is severely tested by losing his livestock, all of his children, and all but one of his servants to bring the news of Job's losses. And if these trials weren't enough to bring the man to his knees in utter despair, a second physical test is on layaway for him.

"So Satan went out from the presence of the Lord and afflicted Job with painful sores from the soles of his feet to the top of his head" (Job 2:7 NIV).

Some would say Job must have sinned against God to bring such calamity on his household, or perhaps he didn't have enough faith to believe God for victory. On the contrary, Job was a man of God. In fact, Job 1:8b declares, *"There is no one else like him; he is blameless and upright, a man who fears God and shuns evil."* The Lord Himself makes this declaration. So what was it that caused this horrible valley experience in Job's life? It was the very fact that he served God with all that he had. Job feared God and served Him, and the enemy of Job's soul was allowed to try him and test him. Notice I said, "allowed."

God allows us to go through difficult times just as he did with Job. Some trials are more difficult than others, but we can choose how we will respond in each instance. Job chose to respond in a God honoring way. Job 2:10b states, *"In all of this, Job did not sin in what he said."* In the chapters that follow we see a man in utter pain and a sense of despair like no one I have ever known. His wife and friends had their own ungodly counsel for him, and he comes to a depth of despair that none of us would ever dare to encounter. The depth of Job's valley seemed bottomless. And like us, Job came to a place where he was worn down physically, emotionally, and spiritually, and there appeared to be no one there to comfort or encourage him. Have you ever been there? In your valley experience, have you come to a place where you feel all alone, worn out and in despair? It is at these places where the enemy of our soul loves to get his hooks in us. He loves to kick us when we're down. But just hold on. There is someone who will never leave us stuck in the bottom of a seemingly bottomless pit of despair. It is the God who made heaven and earth. It is our Creator. It is the One who formed us from nothing, and everything under heaven belongs to him. Chapters 40 and 41 of Job clearly bring Job back to an awareness of who he is in the light of who *He* is. Job repented before the Lord. And the end of the story is far better than it began.

"The Lord blessed the latter part of Job's life more than the first" (Job 42:12a).

The story of Job's valley experience is just one of many biblical examples and from it we can learn: (1) Fear God no matter what or whom comes our way. The deepest valleys demand Godly counsel and close friends who will point us to the Lord for help. (2) How we respond will determine the outcome. We can grow bitter or better from our valley experiences. Draw close to the Lord. Don't run away, for if you do, you'll find it to be a lonely place. (3) No matter what we go through, He is there and desiring to bless us.

So many people picture the Lord as a god who just likes to see people squirm when they go through difficult times. This picture is clearly not the case. God does not delight in seeing people hurt or hurting people. He is all powerful, and desires to come alongside those who will call out to Him in an hour of distress. And lest we forget, He *always* has a plan, and it's never a plan to harm or destroy us.

The following story is our personal experience while my wife Robin and I served as lead pastors of a small, rural church in Colorado for four years (2007-2011). You will read some of our actual journal entries as we were encountering our deepest valleys. It is our prayer and desire that the pages that follow will bring honor and glory to the One who will one day be victorious forevermore over every deep valley we walk through and help those who may going through some dark days even now as you read, *Through the Valley.*

CHAPTER 1

The Valley Begins

My wife Robin and I have had our share of unique valley experiences throughout our lives. Like many people, we have worked through trials, learning from each instance to bring glory to the Lord and take us to a place of deeper learning and dependence on Him. While we don't enjoy going through those trials, we can remember and reflect to see how the Lord brought us through tough times. Our perseverance has made us better people.

Our journey began in the latter part of 2006 while discerning and sensing the Lord was moving us back out into full-time vocational ministry after a seven year break. We sensed a change was coming to our lives but did not know what the next four years would hold or how deep the valley would descend, and I'm grateful to the Lord for His minute-to-minute plan in our lives. To make a long story short, we began to pray about the direction God was taking us and where He would lead us.

While we were living in Missouri, Robin began to experience some physical symptoms that would prompt her to seek a doctor's advice. She called to schedule an appointment with a specialist, and as is the case most of the time, she could not see the doctor right away. She put her name on the waiting list hoping to be seen before we moved. We wanted to stay close to Springfield, Missouri, where our children and grandchildren were, and so we began to search for a place of ministry nearby. Nothing seemed to open to us, and our perfectly planned ministry scenario began to fail. We have a small magnet reminder in our home that says, "We plan… God Laughs!" Isn't that the case most of the time? We plan a scenario that seems to be in our best interest. But God has other plans which include far more than our selfish desires.

I searched for open churches and sent out resumes while praying for His will in the direction He wanted us to go. Robin continued to have symptoms; still no doctor appointment. Nothing opened within 500 miles. So I set our sights on Colorado. I followed the procedure for finding open churches in our Assemblies of God Fellowship within Colorado, and a small church in the southeastern part of the state possessed qualities that attracted us. I inquired about the church, and the doors to La Junta, Colorado, seemed to open. We interviewed, were invited to preach, and in April 2007 were elected to become the pastors in this rural High Plains town. Although elected, it was our desire to know for sure that God was leading us in this direction, and we continued to pray and seek His will concerning this position, for it would be a life-changing event. It would be the first position in our ministry history without our three children beside us.

We returned from Colorado to Missouri with a new sense of direction but still needed some time to consider this move. We asked the congregation and district officials for forty eight hours to pray and contemplate the move. The board agreed, and for the next forty seven hours, we prayed, were counseled, and finally came to a decision which would ultimately change our lives forevermore. We agreed to accept the position and settled on a June move. This would give us some time to pack and wrap up in Missouri. As the June date approached, Robin's doctor's office called with a June appointment, and she simply told them we were moving, and would have to follow up with a new doctor in Colorado in a few weeks.

The move went as well as any long distance move does go. We began our ministry in a new setting not knowing what challenges lie ahead, but we were filled with anticipation of what His power and presence would do through us in this new place. A few weeks passed as we began to get settled, and Robin had secured an appointment with a local doctor, but again, could not get an appointment for several months. This was not what we desired, as she was continuing to present with symptoms that did not appear to be minor. We prayed and waited for the October appointment to arrive. We went on in our ministry responsibilities from week to week as we sought the Lord on Robin's behalf. October finally arrived, and we were anxious to find out what was causing Robin so much physical difficulty the last six to seven months. She met with the doctor and made a decision that a colonoscopy was in order. Robin was forty-seven-years-old at the time, and as is the case under normal circumstances, a colonoscopy is not suggested by the medical community until age fifty. The severity of the situation prompted a quicker response time, and the procedure was scheduled within a week or two.

Our daughter Heather moved to Colorado with us in the first year to help us get settled and aid other areas of ministry. She was especially helpful with areas which neither of us were proficient in like computer issues. On the day of the scheduled procedure, Heather was out of town visiting family and friends back in Missouri, consequently not being able to be at the hospital with her mom and me, but we assured her we would call with the results as soon as we knew something. We walked into our small, regional hospital for the outpatient procedure that would be the beginning of what would turn out to be the mouth of the valley. We prayed together for God's will and hand in this procedure, and Robin was prepped for it as I waited at her bedside in anticipation. I kissed her—then the nurse whisked her away.

One of the highlights of living in a place like Colorado is the great Rocky Mountains. The peaks of these majestic mountains can be seen for miles, and it may take you several hours to arrive at the base of the mountain as you approach from a distance. But there are a couple of lessons I've learned about these mountains that would correlate to life in general. First, the highest mountain peaks are barren and cold. As you approach a high mountain, there is what is known as a tundra line. This is where the lush greenery and fertile soil becomes a place of barrenness to the top. It is cold most of the year; the air is thin and snow caps abound in these places. It is beautiful from a distance and a great place to visit, but no one would want to live there. Second, the mountain peaks are places of loneliness. They are places of solitude and loss of reality. Solitude and loss of reality are only tolerable in small doses, for we all must come back to a place of fellowship, friends and the reality of life. We can draw strength in these high places for a moment, but we must come back to the place where we were meant to grow deep roots.

I did not know how deep our roots would grow and the spiritual lessons we would learn as we began to enter that place where the valley begins.

CHAPTER 2

THE UNKNOWN VALLEY

*"… And surely I am **with you always**, to the very end*
of the age"(Matthew 28:20b).

There are times in our lives when a sense of being all alone in a situation can fill our minds while we are in the circumstances at the moment. No matter how super spiritual we may portray ourselves to be, we are simply human beings that go through difficult times of asking that age-old question of our Lord, "Where are you, God?"

Jesus knew this would be the case in the lives of His disciples as He prepared to ascend to the Father. He called them to follow Him from the beginning of his earthly ministry. They had established an earthly bond and relationship that would now be void of His physical presence, and they would need an assurance of His unending presence in their lives on a minute-to-minute basis. Physically, Jesus was confined to one place at any given time, much like us in human form; but now in the Spirit, He can be everywhere with everyone at the same time in any situation. I'm not certain the disciples fully grasped this promise when Jesus said, *"I am with you always, to the very end of the age" (Matthew 28:20b)*. There would now be a sudden void in their lives with his absence. No doubt they were asking, "What now? Where do we go from here?" And Jesus reassures them He would be there, *always*. What exactly does always mean? It means always. It means when we minister to others, He is there. When we feel all alone, He is there. When we walk through the deepest valleys life can bring, He is there. In the darkest night, He is there. In our victories, He is there. He said, *"Always."* This gives us assurance as his disciples. Our God is an ever-present God, a God who upholds us and has compassion for every situation we go through. But there are times when we have to remind ourselves of this all-important immutable fact. We must grasp this truth by faith, for whatever we have need of He is there to comfort, provide, counsel and give wisdom. And we grow spiritually as we sense His presence in the midst of the situation.

He is there, always. As I sat in the small waiting area anticipating the results of Robin's colonoscopy, I didn't know what to expect the outcome to be. Our hope was it would be something minor that could be dealt with minimally. We never want to think the worst in these situations, but there I was sitting in an outpatient room now void of my Robin, who at that very moment was undergoing a procedure that would ultimately change our lives forever. At that point, a sense of loneliness began to close in on me. All of our families are far from this place, and our closest child was more than 600 miles from us.

Forty-five minutes to an hour had passed; the door opened to the procedure room, and Robin was wheeled back to her recovery area. She was obviously tired and still under the effects of the anesthesia. I leaned over her bed and kissed her and asked her how she did. She awakened with tears, and she looked at me through those beautiful big, green eyes and says the words that no one ever wants to hear.

"The doctor says...it's cancer."

I would love to tell you at that moment I was filled with a deep sense of peace and became a great stalwart of the faith. But my heart sank. Our world, Robin's world, had just been turned upside down in an instant. With one test, one diagnosis, the valley descended miles deeper.

As I held her hand, I tried to fight back the tears and reassure her that this diagnosis did not take God by surprise, and even in it He had a plan. I did not know what that plan was, but God did have a plan. What was it, God? Please, tell me now. I had been by the bedside of many parishioners who had gone through difficult times, but this was now the dearest person to me on the planet. What could I say that would not only help her but bolster my own faith? This was *my* house.

The doctor came out in a few moments with pictures of the procedure and simply told us he had seen this before. He was sure it was colon cancer, but it would have to be confirmed. As I looked at the pictures, I will never forget the ugliness of what I was seeing for the first time. I managed to keep my emotions in check for the moment, and asked the doctor what he suggested. He simply stated a surgery was in order and would have to be done soon. My mind was reeling. Robin was still in and out of sleep catching every other word. He said he would be in touch with our primary care doctor and give her the report. He wished us well and exited. I felt many emotions in those moments. Shock, anger, and a sense of utter helplessness enveloped my heart and mind in a matter of seconds. The questions came.

"What now?"

"Where do we go from here?"

"Do we stay in La Junta?"

"How will we pay for a very necessary surgery without medical insurance?"

These gritty questions began to permeate my thoughts and my mind ran way ahead of the present realities, a side effect when I need answers quickly. It was obvious to me that no answers or very few could be answered now. Time would have to tell what the outcome would be, and I didn't care much for this scenario. We had just been given a cancer diagnosis. We'd been touched by cancer in many lives around us, including loved ones. For the first time, though, we stood in this small regional hospital far from family and heard the words no one ever wants to hear come home to roost on our doorstep. Time seemingly stands still in moments like this as your mind tries to grasp the reality of what just happened. Could it be? Am I dreaming? So many questions. Few answers.

I stepped out of the room and allowed Robin to rest and recover from the anesthesia while I made terribly difficult phone calls to our children and relatives. Our children were as shocked and disheartened as us we were. Questions began to arise from each of them for which I had few answers. All of them agreed to pray, seek God, and try to reassure me of His abiding presence. These moments, what I call "The Return on the Investment," begin to shine through our children. We've taught our children to rely on the Lord for all we need. We've taught them to trust Him through every situation. Now I'm the one who heard it come through the phone back to me as I've just told each of them, "Your mom has colon cancer." The next call I had to make were to my in-laws in Pennsylvania. They have always taken every matter to the Lord, but again, this time it was too close to home. We cried as I told them the news. They asked how Robin was doing, but without fail, they immediately went to prayer on the phone. I assured them I would keep them informed as we made plans for surgery, and we hung up.

Robin was awake now and able to contemplate leaving the hospital. These were solemn moments as we walked down the corridor of the hospital and out to the parking lot. The reality of what just transpired was now beginning to take hold, and at this point I didn't know how all of it would come together. We did not have health insurance, and a surgery like this would be costly. What would be the outcome? I've known many people who dealt with colon cancer, and it was rarely a good outcome. The short drive home was quiet, and our hearts were filled with anticipation and questions that only God could provide answers for.

As we returned to our little home on the east side of town, I got Robin inside and made her comfortable, as she was still feeling the side effects of the anesthesia. We talked briefly about calling her primary doctor to make an appointment but didn't know much beyond that at this point. How would I tell the church? How would they respond? We simply could not think about resigning as we'd only been here four months and Robin needed to have necessary surgery. We discussed the inevitability of an announcement to our church and made plans to tell them the following Sunday.

We called Robin's primary doctor and made an appointment for the next week. A week seems like a month sometimes, and this was one of those times. The anticipation was growing, and we desired to get the answers to the obvious questions.

Sunday came, and I proceeded to lead our Sunday service as usual. It was a difficult service in that my heart was hurting for my wife knowing what she was facing, and I had to lead her and the congregation through this valley in faith, believing God had this all under control. I waited to tell them of her results until the conclusion of the service. There was deep concern and pure love exhibited as I announced the news of her cancer. People began to rally around her and pray. This was now a valley they would walk through with us, and they would come alongside us to uphold us. We would grow and learn together.

As we met with the primary care doctor that next week, we discussed the findings from the colonoscopy and how it needed to be dealt with. This was an ugly malignant tumor in Robin's descending sigmoid colon, and her only hope was to surgically remove it. Our doctor expressed her condolences and referred us to a surgeon in Pueblo, Colorado, where we might find the help we needed.

It was easy to become anxious with each passing moment, and the anxiety was beginning to weigh in on us. It consumed our daily lives. Nearly every thought was this cancer and the effects on our lives from here on out. We knew this cancer inside Robin's body was like a ravaging beast wanting to completely take control, and we wanted to eradicate it as soon as possible.

We wasted no time in securing an appointment with the surgeon as soon as we could see him. As we drove the seventy-five-mile drive to Pueblo that day, we prayed, talked, and listened to music with so many questions, but few answers at this point. All we were sure of was that God was in control of everything we were experiencing and even in this situation, somehow He had a plan. It's easy to give advice about such things, and it's easy to watch people deal with issues like this from afar and pray for them, and not have to deal with the issues personally, but it was our turn now to dig deep into our faith and believe God for His perfect plan in the midst of this valley. Faith was not just a biblical concept. It was knowing God is Who He says He is, and we must trust Him. This was where we had to put working faith into action and not just talk the talk. Little did we realize how much we would learn to trust Him in the future.

As we entered the lobby of the surgeon's office, we saw several people sitting there as we checked in. We were new at this. Some of them looked as if they had been down this road a few times and were veterans. The looks on some of their faces didn't fill my heart with much hope, as some were thin, others grimacing in pain. But nonetheless, we were all in this boat together. Robin filled out the necessary paperwork, and we waited. It wasn't long before we were ushered down the hallway into an examination room. We were getting closer to a plan.

The surgeon came in and introduced himself. As he spoke, we were amazed at his confidence and plan of attack on this beast. He was hopeful. I noticed, though, that throughout the visit he never once discussed how we would afford such a surgery. So I simply addressed the issue before we scheduled. I told him we did not have medical insurance and frankly did not know how we could pay for this service. His response literally brought tears to my eyes as he said, "We will discuss that later, but for now, your wife is very sick, and we've got to get her well." Money was *not* the defining issue for him. Praise the Lord! My heart leaped within me and tears began to flow from my eyes, because I knew in that moment the Lord had put us in the right place. Such a sense of peace overshadowed us at this moment. God obviously orchestrated this encounter. I'm not sure the doctor fully understood what was happening in my heart, but he knew we were obviously moved to tears. The surgeon described how he would perform the surgery, and we said that it would need to be done sooner rather than later. The surgery was scheduled for November 7, just a few weeks away. As we drove the seventy-five-mile trek back home that evening, our hearts were filled with anticipation, and Robin needed some assurance that God would be gracious to her and spare her life.

As we listened to a music CD in our car, a worshipful scripture song began to play which ministered to both of us in a powerful way. But it touched Robin in a more specific way as she held on to the promise in Psalm 118:17: *"I will not die but live, and will proclaim what the LORD has done."*

The presence of the Lord overwhelmed us both as we drove and played that song over and over. We wept, tried to sing and pray as we drove home, and His presence filled our car like never before as we worshiped, as we sensed His abiding presence with us. He would lead us through this valley. The remainder of the trip home was one of thankfulness and praise, and Robin made calls to our children and her parents to inform them of her surgery schedule.

The *"Unknown Valley"* was becoming clearer in what we could see with our mortal eyes, and we had the assurance that He would be with us in what we could not see, *Always.*

CHAPTER 3

GROWING DEEPER

"In my distress I called to the LORD; I cried to my God for help.
From his temple he heard my voice; my cry came before him,
into his ears" (Psalm 18:6).

I have always believed in the power of prayer. I've spent many hours in prayer, I've counseled others for the need of prayer in their lives in communicating with our Lord in an intimate way. I've preached countless times on the absolute necessity of prayer if we are going to see anything accomplished in our lives and in the lives of those around us. I've prayed in nearly every venue I can think of because I know prayer simply demonstrates our finite dependence on an infinite God. Prayer is more than a few words at bedtime. It's more than being thankful at mealtime. Prayer for me is recognizing my need for an intimate relationship with the One who has ALL the answers to every question ever asked and a plan for every scenario before it exists. Moreover, prayer is simply talking with God. That's big.

I've always been impressed by the biblical examples we have to learn from. These were men and women who were just like us in every way. They've felt what we felt and went through relative scenarios as we do. The Lord allowed us to see these examples in order that we understand these people had emotional distress, physical maladies, spiritual needs and every other human need, but the biggest lesson we see from these examples is how they dealt with their plight and who supplied their needs. The Bible always points us to the God who supplies every need without fail.

David was one such individual who captured my attention for many years. He went through some of life's most horrific circumstances. He brought some things on by himself, but other situations came from the hands of his enemies. When I read the Psalms, I heard the joys, fears, hopes, victories, and anguish of a man who had a heart after God. He was a man. A man we all relate to on some level. For me, this fact was reassuring and brought me a sense of peace to know a man like David went through some greater difficulties on occasion, and God was merciful and gracious to him. I found this to be the case as the news of Robin's cancer and pending surgery sent me to my knees on her behalf. I've prayed for my wife before, but the Lord took me to a desperate, deeper place of prayer than I had ever been on her behalf.

We had an upper bedroom and a lower bedroom in our small house, and the lower bedroom made for a peaceful place of prayer in the way it was set up. It would become my prayer closet, as I prayed and groaned before the Lord for my Robin. I remember thinking about David's heartfelt pleas before the Lord on different occasions, and how we read of the anguish we sense in those prayers. He simply poured out his heart before God in ways that cause us to grasp a sense of the pain he was going through in the moment. I had not done it prior to Robin's diagnosis and pending surgery, but I took my Bible, opened it up to the Psalms, and began to pray the Psalms as if I had written it.

My heart was moved in ways I cannot describe.

For hours I lay before the Lord and prayed what David prayed and then would customize those words to include Robin. I toiled in prayer and cried out to Him to spare my wife from the fowler's snare. On-and-on I prayed deep into the night. Did I hear an audible voice? Did a special, glorious, illuminated figure walk into my room? That makes for a spectacular scene, but it did not happen. What did happen was a supernatural presence of the Living God met me there that night. A sense of peace came over me, and I knew He had heard my cries for help as I prayed the scripture. I knew in my heart now that whatever would come of this diagnosis, it would be okay. It would be okay, for the Lord was in control. Whether He had a plan to physically heal her or eternally heal her, I did not know, but I did know we'd have to trust Him.

Little did I realize as I was praying that Robin was praying upstairs and struggling to overcome fear and a heavy-weight fight with the enemy that would cause her to physically tremble from head-to-toe. The enemy loves to come at us in the still of the night when all is quiet, and we are trying to rest. It would become our battleground in the months to come. He would present us with lies and fear, and we would counter attack in prayer and the Word. We didn't how deep our spiritual roots were growing as a foundation for the days to come.

Our children, Robin's parents and two of her sisters all flew in from Pennsylvania, Delaware, and Missouri to pray and support us as Robin and I got ready for the big day.

November 7 arrived, and we prepared ourselves for the unknown as we drove to the hospital and checked Robin in for her surgery. Our hearts were filled with the usual anxiousness that comes with any medical procedure, but this one was different from any other surgery Robin had ever faced before. This surgery would determine our future, perhaps. But whatever the outcome, we were spiritually ready.

Robin was prepped, we prayed, and it wasn't long before the surgery team was wheeling her back to the operating room (OR) to begin a surgical procedure to remove this "thing" in her body. There was nothing left to do now but pray and wait. We were overwhelmed with support from our parishioners, other pastors, and some friends who came to wait it out with us and pray. We were the largest group in the waiting area that day.

Several hours passed, and it seemed like the usual eternity when you have a loved one under distress. Nearly four hours later the doctor came to talk with me and give me a report. He said he had removed eighteen inches of her colon, a section of lymph nodes, the blood supply in the area with it and had clear margins. My next question to him was one Robin and I were extremely concerned about and had taken before the Lord as a concerning prayer.

"Doctor, did she require a colostomy?" His answer brought delight to me instantly, and I knew this was an answer to prayer.

"No", he said, "because of where the tumor was, we had enough colon to reattach it."

He did not feel she would have any other further complications, as the cancer was contained in her colon. This was great news and I thanked him with tear-filled eyes, hugged his neck, and he left. As I look back on my emotional state, he must have wondered about me as every time he said something, it drew tears to my eyes. If the cancer had been lower in her colon, a colostomy would be in order. Praise the Lord. God was answering prayer.

As Robin was recovering in the hospital, she was determined to allow God to use this physical battle as a testimony to others around her. True to form, she had a captive audience. She began to develop relationships with her kindness and gentleness while the nurses and attendants helped her on a daily basis. She testified of the Lord's goodness even while being diagnosed with a cancer that does not go well for many people. A few of the nurses came into her room and one even commented about how bright her room was. Several nurses always seemed to congregate there as time would permit, and they began to develop a relationship that led them to ask her questions. Robin's testimony of His goodness was attractive, and it wasn't long before she was leading one young lady in a prayer of salvation. God would receive the glory in this no matter what the enemy tried to do.

Prior to Robin's surgery, we had committed to giving God the glory in this trial and trusting Him no matter what took place. We realized He had a plan even in this, and we were just a small part of a much larger plan. When we commit our lives to the Lord, it is then that He requires our lives of us. We are no longer steering and directing our lives but simply allowing the Lord to direct our paths. The path may be painless at times, but sometimes it may require a painful experience for one simple reason. That reason is Jesus' entire earthly mission which still stands today.

"For the Son of Man came to seek and to save what was lost" (Luke 19:10).

We were being put to the test in our commitment. Would we become selfish in our physical struggle and feel sorry for ourselves, or would we allow God to use this in our lives as a testimony of His greatness and exhibit His grace in the midst of the valley? We chose the latter, and God honored our obedience.

On another occasion as I came to visit Robin, one of our parishioners was on the same floor visiting a man she knew from our town who had colon cancer and was not expected to survive. She told us his story and asked if I would go down to his room and pray with him, for she didn't believe he had a relationship with Jesus. I was more than happy to oblige, and our parishioner, my daughter and I went to his room in the next few moments. His family was there, and my parishioner introduced me as her pastor—the patient's name was John. I explained that my wife was just down the hall and just had colon cancer surgery as well. I answered their questions about how she was doing and began to give glory to the Lord for what He was doing in our lives through these difficult circumstances. The conversation began to focus on eternity, and it wasn't long before John was praying a simple prayer of salvation and giving his heart to Christ.

This was number two, and the Lord was taking us to that place beyond ourselves, a place that can only come as a result of saying, "Yes, Lord, I'll go where you want me go, and do what you want me to do." We were informed later that John passed away approximately a week after our visit. I don't know why God used us to lead these people to Himself, but I can say it had nothing to do with us. He knew we would be obedient, and He received the glory. It truly comes down to obedience. God will use what you have if you'll give Him what you have to use. The Lord is not looking for what we are able to do but what we are willing to do in spite of ourselves. He's searching for people who will be humbly obedient and depend on Him for everything.

Robin was released from the hospital to begin her recovery process at home. We will never forget how blessed we were when we arrived home to find that some of the ladies from our church had cleaned and gone grocery shopping for us. What a blessing they were to us. The recovery was slow going, as Robin would require help lying down and getting up, and this was a special time for us as we grew closer together in our relationship. Robin comes from a large family and one of her four sisters, Sherrie, from Delaware came to stay and help with Robin and the ongoing daily duties around the house. We were so grateful for her help. We thanked God for walking into this valley with us and helping us to plant deeper roots in Him.

As the weeks progressed, Robin became stronger, and her follow-up doctor visits were positive. We owed a debt of gratitude to our daughter, Heather, who came to live with us the first year we were in Colorado. She could have stayed in Missouri but felt like she needed to be with us. At first it was unclear what her role would be in our lives. But God, in His ability to know the future, knew that Heather would be a blessing to us in aiding with Robin's recovery and church work.

As time passed, Robin continued to have follow-up visits with her doctor. All was going well, and we were praising God for the good reports. On the church front, God was moving our small congregation in a direction to buy property and gave us a vision for the future. People were being saved, and we were experiencing a great move in a forward direction. I was very busy in church and community work and began to draw preliminary plans for a new building. The year 2008 was a year of peace for the most part as we focused on new and exciting times in the future. It seemed our physical battles were behind us as Robin's CT scans came back clear.

The Lord had truly allowed us to go to a much deeper place in the spirit. We learned how to connect with the Lord in an intimate and communicative place we had never been to due to Robin's physical trials. Was this the end of a seemingly deep valley for us? Could we now move on to "higher" ground and get on about our Father's business in the church? Only time, continued prayers and follow-up visits with the doctor would tell.

CHAPTER 4

DEEPER STILL

"Not only so, but we also rejoice in our sufferings, because we know that suffering produces perseverance; perseverance, character; and character hope. And hope does not disappoint us, because God has poured out his love into our hearts by the Holy Spirit, whom he has given us" (Romans 5:3-5).

Have you ever walked in a valley? There is a sense of quietness as the hills on both sides close in on you. It is usually a place of growth, as most valleys have a stream or water supply close by, and it is a place of lush greenery. You can't see too far in the distance, as the valley only affords limited sight. When trying to exit a valley you have several options: (1) You can scale the sides and go up which sometimes requires a steep and treacherous climb, depending on the terrain; (2) you can continue on through the valley and uncharted territory, or (3) turn and go back the way you came. Scaling the rough terrain to escape the valley isn't always easy and sometimes leads to more climbing. Continuing on through the valley will bring you new discoveries and experiences and eventually lead to an exit, but it's an unknown destination. If you choose to turn around and go back the way you came, you forfeit all opportunity for new discovery, growth, and exploration. It will lead to the safe and comfortable place you knew so well.

I grew up deer hunting the hills and valleys of Pennsylvania. I remember hunting in places on mountains where I could see for miles and miles. I also remember climbing down the hillsides into valleys. Once I got to the bottom, I realized it may not have been the best option for me because being in the valley limited my abilities from a hunting perspective. I couldn't see very far. If I were successful in bagging a deer in the valley, who would in the world would want to wrestle it back up the steep sides to get it out to the vehicle? If I chose to go through the valley, I didn't know where it might lead. On one such occasion, I recall being in the bottom of a deep valley that seemed to be so close on both sides you could almost touch them. It was central Pennsylvania, and I didn't know the topography or terrain too well. I remember looking up on both sides of me, surveying a very steep climb if I wanted to go back up. That option was out of the question since I just came down. I chose to walk it out to discover where it would lead me. I felt safe there, for the valley walls gave me a sense of security.

I walked for what seemed an eternity, but I noticed as I walked and carefully climbed over the rocky terrain, the valley began to widen, and eventually it opened up to the most beautiful sight. I lay my eyes on a lush, green, sun-filled, expansive meadow that I didn't know existed. The only way I could have known this beautiful, rich field existed was to walk through the valley I had just come through. It required risk on my part. It required tenacity and the willingness to go into the unknown. I did not get a deer that day, but I learned valuable lessons that would guide me into the spiritual understanding I needed later on in life.

Great anticipation of better days ahead filled us as 2008 began. Robin required rest and limited activity from her surgery. We were hopeful with each new follow-up doctor visit, as it resulted in an encouraging word from her doctor about her recovery process and ongoing prognosis. He was hopeful as well with each result from her CT scans and colonoscopy, all of which continued to show no disease progression. Even though the doctor (surgeon) was hopeful about her ongoing prognosis, he recommended she begin seeing an oncologist for further evaluation and possible chemotherapy treatments as a preventative measure. Robin was not too keen on this idea, but we wanted to look at our options and make informed decisions. We took the surgeon's advice and set a date with the oncologist.

As we entered the oncologist's office that very first visit, it was startling to see the number of people in the waiting area all dealing with some form of cancer or another and all on a different level of care. We were anxious about the outcome of this visit. We were entering another unknown part of this valley. Would chemotherapy treatments be the best option, as Robin did not currently show evidence of disease progression?

We were led to an examination room where in a few moments the doctor came in and introduced himself. As he looked at the file of Robin's medical history, he was impressed to see she had no disease progression in the lymph nodes or other organs, but he encouraged her to begin a chemotherapy regimen as a way of keeping the cancer from returning. He could not make guarantees, however, as he had nothing to gauge progress on. We already knew that about cancer recurrence but had to ask the question. We were left to make a decision now, but the doctor said we could make that decision on our own and would not pressure us. We left his office with having to weigh our options now. I did not want to make a decision for Robin but would encourage her in whatever decision she made to stand by her. I thought about what I might do in her situation, but the fact of the matter is we just don't know what we would do unless we are in one's shoes. We took it before the Lord in prayer. This would be a difficult decision that could have a positive outcome, or it might not. It's a difficult place to be in, as you unpack all of the information and try to make sense of it all. We prayed for wisdom. We counseled with trustworthy, Godly people, but ultimately it came down to Robin making the final decision.

As we prepared for her next visit to the oncologist, Robin was ready to give him an answer concerning her pending treatment options. She refused chemotherapy treatment but decided to try boosting her immune system through dietary means. She felt the Lord had given her peace about making this decision, and the doctor was not real comfortable with this but accepted her decision just the same. We left her decision now in God's hands.

As the months progressed, Robin grew stronger, and she began to get back to helping in the church again and working with the children. We were rejoicing that Robin was feeling better and all seemed well. Christmas came and went, and we entered 2009 on a high note. Her surgeon was pleased, and so was her oncologist.

As we entered January 2009, we were just finishing up the final details on purchasing land for the church where we would build a new facility in the future. We had gone through what seemed to be a forever land and/or building search process, and finally God blessed us through a realtor friend who personally owned a wonderful tract of property on the west side of town. We closed on the property in February of 2009, and we were excited to see all God had in store for our little church. Meanwhile, we had our present facility listed for sale with the intentions of either moving into a transitional venue or begin building as the Lord brought in the funds. We had many prospects and a few offers on the property, but it was just not selling. This New Year began with hope and great excitement, as we were progressing on all fronts, except for this one. More importantly, God was blessing us with new converts. It was a busy season in our lives, and we treasured those moments.

Robin continued to enjoy a positive CT scan and exam during the first two months of 2009. Her surgeon was still hopeful, as she was now nearly a year and a half away from her original diagnosis and surgery. As we entered late spring, Robin began to develop a specific abdominal pain that seemed to be consistently troubling her. She reported this to her surgeon who was a proactive doctor and thought it best to get another CT scan, as it had been several months now since her last one. He scheduled the scan, and we again were hopeful it might be adhesions or something minimal. In the past, Robin reacted to the contrast dye they gave her for the scans, thereby causing her to be pre-medicated several days before each one. The day of the scan came and we were anxious for the positive result. No news came. A day or two had passed, and we still did not hear any news.

Robin called her doctor's office to see if the results were back yet. The doctor called back with concerning news, news we had not anticipated. He said the scan revealed a lesion on her liver. The lesion could be something they didn't see on previous scans, or it could be a benign lesion. At any rate, he did not feel it was something to be concerned about at this time but advised us to keep it under surveillance over the next few months to see if there is any change in size.

This was something we did not want to hear a second time just after coming through what we considered a season of peace. What were we facing here? Again, we tried to be great examples of faith believing God and praying for a miracle. We would tell ourselves, *you don't know what it is. It could be nothing. Scar tissue, a benign lesion that will be of no consequence.* The fact of the matter was, once you know growth is there after going through one cancer surgery, you just can't get it out of your head. The enemy plays on that. Fear can and will overcome you if you don't stay in the presence of God. I was trying to reassure

Robin that God would help us through this, and there was no use in getting upset over something we didn't know.

Once again, we made phone calls to our two sons and daughter informing them of the scan results. And again, they agreed with us in prayer that God would help us and not to worry. Robin made the call to her parents, and true to form, they began to pray and intercede on our behalf. In fact, as the news of this scan result began to spread, we knew we were being covered in prayer in many areas of the country. This was reassuring as our names were being brought before the throne of grace. Knowing people were praying bolstered our faith. Prayer during this time held our arms up in the midst of the battle.

Several months passed, and Robin was scheduled for another scan to see if this lesion had changed at all. She was pre-medicated as usual, prepared for the scan, and off she went a day later. Our hearts were once again filled with what is commonly known in the cancer patient world as "scanxiety," waiting for the results of the scan. A day or two went by as we tried to patiently wait for the news of any change. The call finally came, and the doctor was not so optimistic this time. He informed us the lesion had grown in size. Because of the growth and change in shape of the lesion, he advised Robin to have a liver biopsy for further clarification. She was not too pleased with this news, and I tried to encourage her. It's easier being on the sideline being an "encourager" than it is to actually get in the game and take the hits. But my wife of twenty-seven years was my best friend, my lover, my world outside of my love for the Lord, and she was hurting. Seeing her hurt caused me to hurt.

I tried to focus on my church ministry and community ministry with two different chaplaincies, but my mind was deeply concerned and burdened for my Robin. Again, questions began to invade my brain. And my concern now grew to a deeper level than ever before as I thought back on memories of my mother, who passed away from liver cancer in 1984. I would later find out Robin was concerned and praying for me because she knew my mother's loss was hard for me. She didn't want to see me go through it again with her cancer.

The liver biopsy was scheduled as soon as it could be done, and we braced ourselves for the outcome. The day arrived and we drove the all too familiar seventy-five-mile journey to the hospital. We checked in, and Robin was prepared for the outpatient biopsy. Once again we prayed and put this situation in His hands with all of the trust we could muster in our Lord, knowing He does all things well. Robin was called, and off she went to yet another procedure. My heart was heavy for her as I sat in the waiting area. I prayed. My mind contemplated what I would do or say to console her this time if the outcome was not good.

She emerged from the procedure approximately an hour later, and I was standing in the hallway when she came out on a hospital bed. As she is being taken back to the outpatient recovery area, she began to cry out in excruciating pain. What was happening? I asked for an explanation and was told a liver biopsy transfers pain outside of the biopsy area in the liver, and it can be quite painful. Robin's abdominal muscles were contracting from the pain, thus causing her such tremors that she could not lie still. It was unbearable for me to witness my wife going through this kind of pain from a "simple" procedure. I prayed for her and tried to comfort her. Nothing I could do or say would help her. I felt so helpless in those moments. Soon, a nurse brought her some medication that helped her to calm down and the pain subsided. It wasn't long and she was stabilized enough to go home, but she had to be careful with her activities.

Again we waited for the result of this test now, which would determine many things in our lives. As in the past, the doctor called us in a day or two to tell us the news we had been waiting to hear, whether good or bad. The result was a benign lesion, great news. And being proactive, he suggested another biopsy in a few months to be sure. We thanked him and hung up. We sighed a big sigh of relief, and thanked the Lord for this good news. Our children and family members were as elated as we were with this new result, and we couldn't wait to shout it from the housetops. We gave God the glory and announced the result to our congregation the following Sunday.

The Lord was taking us to a deeper, much deeper place of trust and total dependence in Him, as we were being led to a much deeper place in our faith than ever before in our lives. Would this be the depth of the valley we would have to endure? Only time would reveal the answer to this question, but for now, we were rejoicing in the good news.

CHAPTER 5

A TRUE LESSON IN TRUST

"Trust in the LORD with all your heart
and lean not on your own understanding;
in all your ways acknowledge him,
and he will make your paths straight"
(Proverbs 3:5-6).

We have flown many miles domestically and internationally. Every time we enter an airline terminal to fly to a new destination and walk down the jet way to board the flight, I still get a bit nervous. I'm confessing for the first time here in this written work that I reserve a small amount of doubt in the ability of the airline, the pilot, and crew to get me safely to my destination. It makes me have a greater appreciation for the risks others took in early flight to get to this point in aeronautics. Those who paved the way to modern flight took risks, yes, but it also took a great deal of faith and trust— faith in their abilities and trust in putting themselves in the contraption they invented. Others had to trust them as well, putting themselves at risk in this new era of transportation. It comes down to trust for all of us when we board an airplane. We have to completely trust the engineers who developed the aircraft, the mechanics who built the airplane, the integrity of the metal used to build it, and the pilot's ability to accurately navigate, take us up, and get us to our destination in a safe and timely manner.

Trust.

We exercise trust every day. We trust the car will start when we turn the key, and we trust electricity will be there to power our homes when we flip the switch. But I have never completely and uninhibitedly been able to trust men. I trust some people in my life much more than others. I trust my wife, my children, and those closest to me in ministry, but let's honestly face the inevitable: people will fail. No matter how much we trust others, we simply cannot negate the fact that people will fail at some point, because we are finite. We are apt to fail because we're people. And when people fail it hurts. It especially hurts us when we see someone fail who was not only trusted but held in high esteem. The blow is lessened if we realize and accept the fact that people can be trusted, but only to the extent of our finiteness.

Robin and I have always proclaimed how much we've trusted our Lord. We've trusted him for material needs, we've trusted him for finances, and we've trusted him for help in leading the church and provision. He can be trusted completely and uninhibitedly, because He is God and we can fully trust Him. We've always been taught about the things God can do, but what about those things He cannot do?

Before you put the book down and proclaim me to be a heretic, allow me to explain. God is God, and He is true to His Word. If He says he'll provide all of our needs according to His riches in glory in Christ Jesus, then we can take Him completely at His Word. Why is this? He simply cannot lie. If He says, "I'll be with you always," as I previously stated, then He will be with us *always*. Something else God cannot do is fail. Failure is not in His character. God is the God of all that is good and right. If we are seeking Him to do that which is in His plan in our lives, and we allow Him to complete His plan, then we must trust Him to do what is in His best interest for our lives no matter what obstacles may come. He is fail-safe.

So, where do we go wrong in trusting Him? Many times, we allow the enemy of our souls to infiltrate what we truly know in our hearts to be trustworthy and true. When we are faced with insurmountable odds and our backs are against the wall, we suddenly allow fear and doubt to creep in, and the enemy causes our fear to become fully blown out of proportion that sometimes to the point where we can't see anything but the closeness of the valley walls with no way out. Desperate measures call for a desperate and a focused plan of attack. When we are overwhelmed with the material and physical cares of this life, we tend to lose our focus on our God and in His abilities. We begin to question, and questioning God's abilities all stem from the human nature we all have because of the fall of man in Genesis chapter 3. It's the age-old question that began with the serpent where the seed of doubt was planted in the hearts of every human being, "Did God really say?" If we begin to doubt His Word, then we will begin to doubt His abilities.

When Jesus was tempted in the wilderness by Satan, even Jesus didn't combat and defeat the enemy with human words. He defeated him with the Word of God. The enemy can be defeated by the Word of God, because it is powerful and sharper than any two-edged sword. So, when we become fearful of those mountainous trials in our lives, we can and should trust completely in His Word and know God will be true to His Word. I know, it's easier said than done when you get a foreclosure notice or a disconnect notice and the bank account is dry. It's easier said than done when the doctor gives you a shocking diagnosis and poor prognosis, but it is here in the valley floor where our faith and trust is tested. What are we made of, and in whom do we trust? We don't trust in men, worldly governments or the systems of men. We trust in the Lord our God. The everlasting God. Maker of heaven and earth. The only One who can save man from his sin and give him eternal life.

The Word says, "Trust in the Lord with all your heart and lean not on your own understanding" (Proverbs 3:5). This simply means trust Him with all our inmost being and don't try to figure God out by human understanding. It can't be done. And then the rest of this Scripture says, "In all your ways acknowledge him, and He will make your paths straight" (Proverbs 3:6). In my interpretation, this means let God be God in your life. Relinquish to Him every part of your life whether or not you perceive it to be good or bad, and He will direct every step as we follow His lead. We were learning to trust God for Robin's medical needs, her physical needs, and every need we had. We were learning to trust God even more in our church attendees, who were watching our lead in how we were dealing with these physical issues. This was truly a lesson in trusting our heavenly Father for all our needs.

As the summer of 2009 turned to Fall, all seemed to be going along well for Robin physically until she began to develop abdominal pains. This was something she was noticing to be a more frequent, constant pain in her midsection. She called her surgeon's office, and they scheduled her for an appointment and exam. We were concerned as the day approached, but we believed God to help us. We prayed. Our family was praying. We left it in His hands and trusted God for the answer.

Our appointment day came, and we were somewhat anxious to talk with the doctor about this "new" development. We discussed the possibility of scar tissue and a few other things. He examined Robin in the area of her pain, and simply didn't know what it could be without another CT scan of the lesion on her liver, as it had been several months since the last one. He wanted to be sure there was no change in the lesion. It was the only way we could tell. We scheduled yet another CT scan and returned home. With Robin's reaction to the contrast dyes used in CT scans, she had to be pre-medicated before this one. The routine was becoming all too familiar to us at this point, but we pre-medicated her the day before and the day of the CT scan. We prayed for a good report and the Lord's perfect will.

Again, we drove to Pueblo, Colorado, to the hospital, checked in, and Robin was called in to have her scan. We would once again wait for the results. We tried not to think too much about what was or wasn't going on in her body, but with this or any cancer you just can't take your eye off of it, and it had been less than two years since her surgery. A day seems like a week when you're waiting for a test result, and this time was no different for us. We waited and prayed.

Finally, the call came from the doctor. The lesion, which was unchanged in the last scan, had now taken on a new form. It was clearly larger, and this was now a concern for us. The doctor was calm and didn't show too much concern, but suggested another biopsy of the liver lesion to be sure. This news did not make us happy, as the pain from the last biopsy was still very fresh in Robin's mind. But once again, we were in a position to trust God for the outcome. We rationalized there was no sense in getting upset over something we were not sure of. God knows all about it and has a plan. We made the usual calls to our family and made the church aware of the next step in this journey. Everyone we knew was praying. This was so important for us to know at this point in our lives. Churches in our district and section were praying. Prayer was the one thing we knew was keeping us strong and enabling to go on through the valley. For the first time in our lives, we could literally feel the strength and peace the Lord was providing us throughout this emotional and stressful time. The Holy Spirit was evidently leading us through this valley, and it was ours to trust Him all the way.

The biopsy was scheduled. We continued to pray and believe God for miracles. The church was standing with us in prayer and being supportive. Our district officials were calling to affirm their love and prayerful support. We could do no more from a human perspective, but it was now in His hands, and we knew He does ALL things well.

We were even more anxious this time as we entered the hospital and checked in for the biopsy. Robin had asked for another doctor to perform this biopsy hoping this time it would be less painful. She informed them of the pain she had from the previous biopsy, and they ordered pain medication in advance this time. The moment arrived, and her name was called. I followed Robin and the nurse back to a waiting room where I could immediately be there when Robin emerged from the procedure. I waited and prayed. I was hurting me to see my wife, the love of my life, going through this again. I fought back the tears and knew I would have to be strong for her when she came out of the procedure.

Thirty or forty minutes passed, and the door opened. Robin was finished, and they were transporting her up to the outpatient area to recover from the procedure and monitor before discharge. As she lay there in the outpatient bed, the look on her face told the tale. She was beginning to have the pain she had experienced after the first biopsy, but this time she felt as if she was going to pass out and nausea had set in. I was trying to console her, and I reported Robin's pain to the nurse. They quickly brought her something for the nausea. That seemed to help the nausea subside, but she was still feeling faint.

Remember, they had pre-medicated her before the procedure to help ease the pain. Everything seemed to be going well, and she asked to use the restroom. This small request turned into a major concern when I saw two nurses running towards the restroom and heard Robin's cry for help. I ran the short distance to see my wife passed out and slumped over. The nurses were calling her name with no response.

I am normally not a reactionary person, but this was my wife and I didn't know what was happening. I held my composure and allowed the professionals to handle this. I suppose if you're going to pass out, the hospital is the best place to do it. In a few moments, Robin had regained consciousness and was making her way back to the bed. My heart sank and the emotions began to take over as a lump the size of a baseball formed in my throat. I was hurting inside and had to step out in the hallway to take a deep breath, regain my composure and re-enter the small recovery area where Robin was now waiting. The radiologist who performed the biopsy was called and told of what just transpired and immediately came to check on her. Robin had never taken a full adult dosage of any medication, and it was concluded that not only did he give her the adult dosage of pain medication, but because of her prior incident, he gave her a little more to be sure. He over-medicated her, thereby causing the side effects she had experienced. He recommended she stay in the hospital overnight for observation to be safe, as we lived so far away. This was a day we did not soon forget. But it was nothing the Lord didn't already know about in His divine omniscience. We were trusting Him.

Robin stayed in the hospital that night, and I was accommodated to be able to stay with her. The night was long but without incident, and she was discharged the following day. Again, we were awaiting the result of this latest biopsy, and again we prayed and sought the Lord for His perfect plan in all of this. These are the times when your thoughts and emotions can truly weigh heavily on you, and it was no different this time as we waited to hear something from the doctor. You try to do the things you know to do while the daily ministry demands continue. In fact, it helps a great deal to be able to minister to others while you yourself are going through difficult times, for the Lord can and will use what we're going through at any given moment in the lives of others if we keep it in perspective and not grow inward.

The Call Came

The call came approximately one week before Thanksgiving. We had just pulled into the mall parking lot when the doctor gave us the news. I took Robin's hand as he spoke.

"This is doctor H. The results are back from your liver biopsy, and it's not the news we had hoped for. The lesion in your liver is malignant."

He tried to be positive, and he proceeded to tell us it was one lesion and could be dealt with surgically. He told us he would be referring Robin to a liver specialist in Denver who was excellent with these types of liver problems and his office would be in touch with us to schedule a consultation. We thanked him and hung up. Could this be happening? Not again! Another cancer diagnosis in her liver? Our minds were spinning. I tried to assure Robin and encourage her once again that the Lord was still in control of this. He knew this was coming before we did, and assured her we'd go through this together. As we bowed our heads in prayer in our car that day, we humbly and brokenly opened our hearts to the Lord. We cried out to Him and gave this new diagnosis to Him. Again, we would move just a bit deeper into the valley with this news, but the Lord was leading us, and that made the difference.

Robin made the all-too-familiar calls to our children and Robin's parents who were all trying to be encouraging, but they were disappointed to hear this latest news. And once again, we had more questions than answers at this point, but all of them assured us they would be praying. It is one thing to receive this news, but it is even more difficult for all involved when you are separated by many miles. It's in times like these when you wish family could be present, but they weren't and the Lord would bring a peace to our hearts to know of His presence. With His help and presence, we could do this, and we could fully trust Him.

CHAPTER 6

A VALLEY OF THREE

*"Even though I walk through the **valley** of the
shadow of death, I will fear no evil, for you are
with me; your rod and your staff, they comfort me"*
(Psalm 23:4)

The closeness of the valley walls can sometimes cause us to
feel a sense of loneliness as we walk through our own, unique
situations. Physical trials are just one aspect of those trying
times that can cause us to feel alone as we walk through life's
uncertainties. Relational issues, emotional trauma, and financial
issues are all relevant hardships we deal with as individual
human beings, and all of these have a measure of depth. For
some, it seems like a bottomless pit with trial after trial. Others
go through some tough times but not to the depth that others
must travel. Only God knows the load each of us can bear, and
He entrusts it to us. The most important benefit in being aware
of this is we are not expected to bear our burdens alone. First
Peter 5:7 says, "Cast all your anxiety on him because he cares
for you." This simply means, "Throw it down." Put whatever

we're going through on Him. Why? Because He cares for you! He knows what we're feeling, thinking, sensing, and every struggle we go through no matter how deep the valley may seem. And He is willing to carry those burdens and walk through the valley with us, upholding us as we go. We should never feel like we're "going it alone" when we deal with life's challenges.

The problems come when we try to carry our own burdens. We simply are not made to carry our own burdens. It is not humanly possible for us to carry such burdens. Jesus went to the cross and paid the price not only for our sin relieving us from the sin burden, but he also took every care life presents to us. This is a most freeing thought as we grasp the reality of it. We are somehow willing to embrace the thought that Jesus is powerful enough to forgive our sins, but we are not willing to think He is powerful enough to carry our burdens. He must be Lord of all and everything in our lives or else He died in vain. This is all inclusive. He desires to be at the center of every joy, fear, anxious thought, trial, testimony and victory.

It was only a few days when the Denver liver specialist's office called to schedule a consultation about Robin's recent cancer recurrence and plan of action. Robin scheduled the appointment, and once again was anticipating this meeting with another doctor. The days seemed like months to Robin, as she now knew cancer was present in her liver, and it had to be dealt with as soon as possible.

The day of the appointment arrived in late December, and we drove the three-hour drive to the Denver hospital to meet with the specialist. As we sat in his office and discussed the surgical procedure, he was confident in his ability to resect this part of her liver with minimal liver removal and be able to remove the cancer. One lesion appeared to be more on the surface of her left lobe of the liver. We talked for a few more moments, scheduled the surgery for January 7, 2010, and left his office with confidence. The Lord had orchestrated this meeting and time, and He would receive the glory in the outcome.

We summoned everyone we knew to pray for Robin, as she was now facing her second cancer surgery in two years. The support we received from neighboring pastors, churches, our district, and other churches in other states was absolutely astonishing, as we saw the body of Christ support us and call on the Lord on our behalf. We will always be grateful for this support, as it provided a great deal of strength to us.

●

The Battle Rages…

We were preparing for Robin's impending surgery on January 7 and doing all we knew to do on the home front. We were between Thanksgiving and Christmas now, and it is always a very busy time for a church and families in general. But the end of 2009 was much different than previous years. We already knew what we were facing going into 2010 with Robin's surgery.

On Sunday morning, December 20, 2009, I arose early as was the norm for me on Sundays. I began to prepare myself for the service in prayer and analyze my sermon. As I entered

45

the restroom to begin my day, I was astounded by a shocking presentation of nickel to quarter-sized blood clots in the stool. I thought was a bladder infection or a bad kidney infection. What I saw simply caused me to be afraid of what might be happening in my body, and I cried out for Robin to come. She was just as shocked, and we could only speculate about what might be happening.

What I was experiencing in my heart and mind was the single most frightening moment I have ever had personally. It seemed to me as if my kidney or bladder was coming apart in pieces before my eyes. I tried to pass it off as an infection and thought to myself, *I'll drink plenty of water and cranberry juice the next few days, and that should flush it out.*

We were blessed to have a male nurse in our congregation, and when I arrived at church, I called him aside and told him about my symptoms to gain his perspective about what it might be. He too, thought it may be a bad infection. He determined that flushing it out was a good option, but I should not prolong seeing a doctor. I agreed and thought I would see a doctor by Tuesday if the symptoms persisted. We went on to have a wonderful service that morning, but the thought of what might be happening in my body was now weighing heavily on my mind like a boat anchor. It was nearly impossible for it to think on anything else. I prayed for this to be just an infection.

Sunday passed and Monday brought the same results in the stool, even as I drank more water and cranberry juice than I thought was possible for any human to consume. I was growing more concerned as the symptoms would continue into Tuesday.

I allowed myself the opportunity most of that day to see if this "infection" would subside. It simply did not subside, and I made the decision to travel the seventy-five-mile drive to Pueblo, where I could be seen in an ER for what I thought would be an antibiotic to get me back to health and go home. I had no unusual pain or other symptoms that would have prompted me to think it was not an infection.

Several months prior to my symptoms, I began waking up in the middle of the night on a nightly basis sweating profusely. By nature, I have always been one that does not tolerate warmer temperatures very well, so sweating was not too concerning for me. But this was different. Heavy perspiration would run from my body, and I knew this was much different from anything I had ever experienced before, but I didn't have a clue what might be causing it. As we entered the ER that evening on Tuesday we had no idea what the next two hours would hold, but we were confident the Lord would help us, as He had brought us this far already.

I registered at the front desk, and it was not long before I was ushered into a room where a nurse would be gathering the information needed to begin this process of diagnosis and recommendation for recovery. I informed her of my symptoms over the past two days, and my self-help cure of added fluids to flush it out. She took my vitals, assured us the doctor would be in shortly and exited the room.

As I lay there on the examination bed and Robin sat beside me, I remember thinking and telling Robin, "This shouldn't take long. We'll get a prescription and be on our way."

A few minutes went by, and a female doctor entered the room and introduced herself to us. We chatted a few moments and then she asked me about my symptoms and what brought me in. I reiterated all that been happening, and she ordered a urinalysis and blood work to make a determination. She said she would be back with a report as soon as she received some news and left. Here we were in another very familiar setting at the hospital, waiting for test results, but this time it was me.

Sometime later, the doctor re-entered, and simply said, "I have good news and bad news. The good news is, there is no infection, but there is plenty of blood present in the UA. We'll have to find out where that is coming from, so I've ordered an ultrasound." I agreed, and in a few minutes I was on my way down the hall to a dimly lit room where the ultrasound machine was. The technician scanned me, and ushered me back out to the room where Robin was waiting. Again, we waited for test results. We had absolutely no idea what the findings would reveal, but we did know at least at this point that I wasn't going home with an antibiotic. Robin and I talked about the irony of all of this. She was scheduled for major liver surgery in just two weeks, and here we are in the ER waiting for my test results. It just seemed unbelievable and inconceivable to us.

A knock on the door came within a few minutes, and my doctor entered to tell me they didn't see everything they wanted to see on the ultrasound and thought a CT scan would offer a better look. I agreed, and she said a technician would come and get me soon. At this point, I began to question just exactly what was going on in my body. What were we looking for?

Let's hope it's minor, and I could go home. The minutes now turned into a couple of hours since first entering the hospital, and I was becoming anxious. I tried to tell myself not to get upset about something we didn't know at this point. The CT tech came and ushered me to the procedure room and prepped me for a chest, abdomen and pelvis scan with IV contrast. An IV contrast is used to highlight any area in question in order to obtain a better look at certain areas of our bodies when doing a scan. The CT scan did not take long, and I was once again on my way back to my examination room to rejoin my waiting wife. In these moments of uncertainty, speculation can and does begin to settle in on our thought processes. Robin and I tried to talk about other things. I was physically tired. It was just a few days until Christmas, and we were looking forward to seeing our children and grandchildren who were planning on coming to spend Christmas with us. It would be a wonderful reunion. As most everyone does at this time of the year, we contemplated the gifts we bought and the dinner on Christmas Day. We talked about the upcoming Christmas Eve service at church. We talked until the doctor re-entered the room. She sat down. She looked at us with an eerie seriousness.

"We have the results of your CT scan, and you have a large mass on your right kidney, and it's highly suspicious of renal cell carcinoma."

"What? "How large is it?" I asked.

She responded, "12 centimeters."

"12 centimeters! That's the size of a grapefruit!" I responded.

She confirmed my analogy.

"Ok, doctor, I'm not exactly sure what renal cell carcinoma is. Please clarify."

"It's kidney cancer. And a tumor this size is not good."

The questions began to fill my mind. Cancer? Can we surgically remove it? What's the prognosis? All she said was the prognosis for kidney cancer of this magnitude is generally poor, but I would now have to see a urologist to move ahead with a plan, and she would refer me to several in the city she knew. The doctor offered her condolences and explained she would be right back with discharge papers and the phone numbers. She exited the room.

Our room was filled with a deep sense of disappointment as Robin and I looked at each other with shock. Did we hear this correctly? Are you kidding me? I got up from the bed I had been sitting on, and I began to pace back and forth. My mind began to race. I just received the worst news of my life, besides Robin's first and second cancer diagnoses.

We had fallen into a dark chasm of a valley that was already miles deep.

I responded back and forth between reality and disbelief. "I have cancer? I don't have time for this!" I said to Robin. "This can't be happening to both of us." We were simply numb at this news and shook our heads in disbelief. How could we tell our children both of their parents have been diagnosed with life-threatening cancers at young ages? Where would this valley lead us? I began to think about how we would pay for all of this, as we had no health insurance. Once again, we were facing insurmountable odds.

The doctor came back a few moments later, instructed us, and we were dismissed. This was not the news I came to expect when we left our house. As we drove away from the hospital that night, our hearts and minds were in utter disbelief. We had absolutely no idea how all of this would play out, but we did know we served a God of the impossible. This was an impossible situation for us financially, emotionally, and spiritually. Our Lord would have to carry us through this valley. In times like these, we quickly realize just how small we are in the vast universe and how utterly dependent we are on our Lord. This valley could only be walked with Him leading us. The depth of this valley would take three to get through it!

CHAPTER 7

BETWEEN THE ROCK
AND HARD PLACE

"Don't be afraid, I've redeemed you.
I've called your name. You're mine.
When you're in over your head, I'll be there with you.
When you're in rough waters, you will not go down.
When you're between a rock and a hard place,
it won't be a dead end—
Because I am God, your personal God,
The Holy of Israel, your Savior. (Isaiah 43:2-3, The Message)

When we are faced with insurmountable odds in the flesh,
fear can be a crippling factor even for those who are the most
spiritually astute among us. We'd all like to say how we would
handle ourselves in a situation that would yield a deeply spiritual
and faithful response. But the fact of the matter is, we don't
know how we'll handle any situation until we are face-to-
face with the most difficult hardships life can bring. It can
be an unexpected death, a life threatening physical diagnosis,
relational disruption in divorce or separation, emotional

trauma, or catastrophic financial hardship, to name a few. And fear many times is not negated just because we have a personal relationship with the Lord. Fear is where Satan loves to bring doubt, worry, anxiety and selfishness into play. The Lord makes it known in the Isaiah passage at the beginning of this chapter that He is a *personal* God. Life can be cruel to us at times, but the most important factor to be considered when facing times of deep distress and fear is that He won't leave us between a rock and a hard place with no way out. He is The Rock when we feel like there is no answer and fear settles on us like a dark, ominous cloud. He always makes a way where there seems to be no way. There are no dead ends in His kingdom.

These were the thoughts and promises Robin and I had to immerse ourselves in as we were now in the physical fight of our lives. We knew we could not hold up emotionally or otherwise if we were self-dependent. Our strength had to come from the Lord if we were going to endure the unknown as we faced insurmountable odds.

As we drove home from the hospital on December 22, 2009, the seventy-five-mile trip was a most solemn time for both of us. All I could think about now was getting this "thing" out of my body. I felt as if something foreign, evil and unwelcome had taken up residence in me, and it had to come out. Christmas and New Year's Day were upon us in a few days making it difficult to reach any doctor's; therefore, I would have to wait until after the holidays to begin searching for a doctor to help me. Meanwhile, Robin's liver surgery was the main thought and priority in the coming days, and we had to focus on that. I would not rest until I knew the outcome of her surgery before tackling my own mountainous obstacle.

Christmas was a memorable time for our family. Robin and I were both facing life-threatening illnesses, and we just didn't know the eventual outcome.

Our thoughts were not turned to material gifts and things that would last only for a brief moment in time. Our perspectives changed dramatically. Life itself was now a precious gift. The lives of our children and their families were our focus, and we wanted to spend as much time as we could with them. Two of our three children with their families were able to make the commitment to travel to Colorado to spend time with us, in spite of the fact that they would have to return in a few weeks for Robin's surgery. What a joy it was to have them there and share the excitement of the most wonderful time of the year: the birth of our Savior.

We spent the next few days together trying to focus on each other and share stories and gifts that now had more meaning than at any time in our families' history. These were moments of clarity, as we all knew the next few weeks and months would be trying times for our family and our church.

Christmas came and went, our family returned to Missouri, and we prepared ourselves for the upcoming surgery Robin would have to endure in Denver. So many questions invaded our minds in those days following Christmas with few answers. We not only faced the physical challenges but financial challenges as well. Robin received a phone call from the hospital where she would have her surgery in just a few days with a preliminary scheduling and preregistration. While they had her on the phone, they also informed her of their copay requirement to have the sum of $965 the day of surgery before the surgery could be done. We were astonished to hear this news with just a few days warning. We weren't prepared for this news although $965 wasn't much money considering the type and quality of the surgery she was facing. The point for us was simply: we didn't have the money and did not have the resources to secure it. We felt as if we were being closed in between a rock and a hard place.

This was another teaching and learning moment of faith on the fly, as we had to recall, *"When you're in over your head, I'll be there with you. When you're in rough waters, you will not go down. When you're between a rock and a hard place, it won't be a dead end—Because I am God, your personal God, The Holy of Israel, your Savior."* We once again had to trust Him to supply our need. We weren't asking for a new car, housing or other tangible needs. We were asking for the finances to perform a lifesaving surgical procedure for Robin.

We prayed and were very careful to share the need with just a few close friends. In a day or two, I received another phone call from a friend in our district who asked if we had received the needed money for Robin's surgery to which I responded, "No, nothing yet." We spoke for a few more moments, and he said he had some friends who would be sending us a check in the amount of $965 for Robin's surgery.

We were astonished and blessed, as God had answered our prayers through a source we would never have guessed. He delivered us in our financial hour of need as we made plans to go to Denver. He is The Rock between a rock and a hard place, and He is one hundred percent on time.

The anxiety grew in the next few days as we prepared to go to Denver on January 6. The day came, and we made the three and a half-hour drive while our sons flew in from Missouri and our daughter, Heather, and son-in-law, Josh, came from Iowa to be with us. To add to the already heightened anxiety, they were all on one plane flying into Denver in the midst of a snow storm. As I drove to the airport that night to pick them up, I prayed for their safety. The drive was slow going due to blowing snow and one lane driving conditions. They all made it safely, but it wasn't without incident for Heather and Josh. While driving from Iowa to the Kansas City airport in a blinding snowstorm, they slid off the highway and into a ditch where they became stuck. It just "happened" that a tow truck was behind them to help them and got them back on the road. They just made it to their airport in time, but their flight was canceled due to the storm, and they had to get another flight out. It was the last flight going to Denver.

We stayed at a motel the night before surgery, and as was always the case before a major surgery, sleep does not come easily. Our children were with us, and the bitter cold, snowy January morning was soon upon us as we made the short trip to the hospital in the very early morning of January 7. Robin was facing an uncertain liver resection, but we checked in and prepared to see her off. She told me she was at peace with this surgery. In fact, the Lord had given her an unprecedented peace, unlike her first surgery in Pueblo. The Holy Spirit had prepared her for the unknown. As a nurse was wheeling her into the operating room, Robin was informed for the very first time that they would be resecting up to eighty percent of her liver. Robin was in utter shock, for no one had ever told her this prior to the surgery. She thought it would be much less. Thankfully, this information came just a few minutes before the anesthesia would be administered. As we watched her being wheeled into that OR, we prayed again. And in a few moments Robin was out of sight and in the hands of her surgeon and The Surgeon. This would be another rock-and-hard-place moment, but our hope was in the One who is our personal God.

It was such a wonderful display of love and care as many friends, parishioners, and fellow Colorado State Patrol Chaplains came to sit with our family during the surgery that morning. We were blessed to have them there, and we'll never forget the kindness shown to us in our hour of need. This was the body of Christ in action when we could hold up each other's arms in the midst of a battle.

Time spent in a hospital waiting room appears to stand still when someone you love is undergoing surgery, but Robin was out of surgery in approximately three to four hours with a tremendous report. As the surgeons were conferring about her case in the OR, they made a decision to only resect five percent of her liver and scoop out the tumor leaving clear margins. What a wonderful report. Praise God. He heard Robin's cries for mercy and our prayers for His perfect will were completed.

He said, *"When you're in over your head, I'll be there with you."* He came through—again.

The next few days of recovery were not easy for Robin, as she experienced the pain and challenges of recovering enough to make the nearly four-hour trip back home. As she was recovering, I was making contacts with urology referrals given to me by the ER when I was diagnosed back in December. I made an appointment with a Pueblo doctor as soon as possible. Robin was there approximately six days before being discharged to go home. As we left the hospital that day, we were certain God had met us there even though we had to go through some deep places. We were being "built up" in the faith. God may not rescue us from every storm, but He will be in the boat with us, and when Jesus is in the boat, trust Him to calm the storm. He knows all too well how to handle every detail, and we get an opportunity to see Him at work.

CHAPTER 8

A MIRACLE IN THE MAKING

"And my God will meet all your needs according to the riches of his glory in Christ Jesus" (Philippians 4:19).

We all like to claim we believe this verse of Scripture, and we're quick to recite it from memory when we're in need. We are certainly eager to quote it to someone we know is going through a difficult, needy time. We know God is "The God of All Provision," and He will meet our needs. But this is America, land of plenty and independent culture where we don't really have to depend on God for much. It's true. If we have a physical problem, we are blessed with the best medicines and procedures in the world. Food is pretty much in abundance. If we can't pay our bills, there will be some assistance there for us. God in many cases has become a last resort when we truly need Him. Sad but true. I could go on about this very disconcerting truth, but I'll leave that for another day and book. Suffice it to say, my life was about to come face-to-face with a stark reality concerning my future health. Only a provisional God could help me, for my back was against the proverbial wall with seemingly no way out.

Robin was now resting at home and recovering well from her liver resection. She was moving slowly from the abdominal surgery, and she could not lift or do strenuous activities such as clean the house or other daily common household chores. She didn't like the restrictions. I was still ministering at our church, therefore I still had to maintain my responsibilities there and continue to be a help to Robin.

We were so blessed by her sister, Sherry, who came from her home in Delaware to help us and stay with us a couple of weeks during her recovery until I could get the details worked out with my impending doctor appointment and surgery. I made an appointment with one of the referred urologists in Pueblo to begin making plans for my surgery and whatever else he may suggest. I needed to see him quickly, as I cannot convey the anxiety that can build within you when you realize you have cancer growing inside you. The receptionist got me in to see the doctor as soon as she could. My mind was filled with questions that invaded every thought with a cancer diagnosis. Unfortunately, we had been down this road two times with Robin, and I had gotten familiar with some terms.

The day finally arrived for my appointment, and I entered the busy office with questions in hand. The doctor entered the room and introduced himself. He looked over what reports I had from the scans and my trip from the ER several weeks prior. We talked briefly for a few moments, and he simply gave me very little hope. He had never worked on a tumor this size and didn't know anyone in the area who could. What? He asked me if I wanted to see it and took me to his computer to view the CT scan I had undergone a few weeks before. I'm no doctor, but I could clearly see the tumor, as it enveloped my right kidney and pushed up into my liver. It was a shocking sight for me to witness and one that gripped me with questions. Now what? Where do I go? The doctor didn't have a referral for me. I couldn't believe what I was hearing. I was suddenly thrust into a stark reality as I stood there looking at the CT image. We walked back into the exam room with very little to say. The doctor basically left it up to me to find my own answers, scheduled me for a follow-up visit, and I left.

My mind was reeling on that cold winter day as I left his office. The finality of that visit caused me to look at my future in a whole different light. How long did I have to live? Will I see my grandchildren grow up? What will happen to Robin if I go home before her? Where do I begin to look for help? I drove home that day with many unanswered questions. I had been through some very difficult situations with parishioners, and most times I could say the right things and pray with them, but now I felt alone and fear began to invade my mind and heart. I cried as the gravity of this situation seemed to come down on me like a truck load of bricks. My back was against the wall with no way out. It wasn't the fear of dying that gripped me. It was the concern of not being able to get help and dying basically because I didn't have health insurance. I felt as if the valley walls were closing in on me like never before.

My Journey Begins…

I arrived home to tell Robin the news I had just received from my urologist, and now she was in disbelief. I had no options except to begin calling hospitals and specialists who could deal with such a large tumor and specifically renal cell carcinoma (RCC), which narrowed the search. I began my search with the hospital in Denver where Robin had surgery just a few weeks prior. I made the call and was able to get an appointment with an oncology urologist. I made a plea for surgery and was told it would have to be approved by a doctor and board who looks at each case and makes a determination. I was hopeful they would perform my surgery. Again, I would now be waiting to hear if anyone would perform this surgery and whether or not the hospital would allow me to be treated there without insurance. A few days passed as I contemplated the outcome. Finally, the call came. The urologist's office called, and I was informed they had denied my surgery. No. This can't be happening to me. Robin and I prayed and tearfully cried out to the Lord for provision. Lord, please make a way where there seems to be no way.

We shared the news with our children and family, as we were dealing with what seemed to be a stone wall in our lives. The nights were the most difficult for me as darkness fell and I lie down to try to sleep. My mind did not shut down from each day's events and all of the hurtful roadblocks I was running into. I lie in the stillness of the night and literally began shaking as the fear of not getting help enveloped my being. I prayed my way out of these fearful and terrifying moments, and finally the peace and presence of God came and caused me to be able to sleep. I was literally battling in prayer for my life. I remember crying out to the Lord to extend my life as He had done for Hezekiah of the Old Testament.

My thoughts and actions were dedicated to finding a medical facility that would treat my cancer.

I called some of the most notable medical institutions in the United States and was turned down except for one surgeon in another state who agreed to perform my surgery pro bono. But when it went to the financial office for a decision to be performed in this surgeon's facility, I was denied.

I had nearly given up all hope in finding a facility that could help me when I received a call from our daughter, Heather. I didn't know it, but she went on a her own mission to call all over the United States on my behalf to see if she may be able to get me the help I needed. She made a connection with a hospital in Cleveland, Ohio, and spoke to a lady named Linda. Heather explained our situation to Linda, and Linda simply told her she could help us but would need to speak to me to confirm my information. Heather called me to tell me they had agreed to help me, but I would have to call and speak to her. She reiterated the phone number, and I called immediately.

Linda was kind and reassuring. She heard my plea and simply stated to me they were there to help me and would certainly not deny me based on my inability to pay. She said that because they were a foundation, they were able to do things for people some other places could not do. I was shocked and elated. I began to weep on the phone and excused myself from the conversation for a moment. Linda waited for me. I explained to her how I had been denied at every turn, and this was an answer to prayer for me. I even asked her if this was "for real." She assured me it was, and said her scheduler would be calling in a few days to schedule my appointment with my new urologist and surgeon. I thanked her and hung up. I had a new sense of hope now fill my heart in a way I had not felt in a month. I was going to get help. I was going to have surgery, and I was happy. I was overjoyed, and the emotions began to overwhelm me as I shared the news with Robin. We gave thanks to the Lord, cried, and prepared to receive a phone call from Cleveland to schedule me. That was Friday, and I had to wait until Monday to hear from them, but it made my weekend much brighter as I contemplated the next week. I called Heather and share my latest news with her, since she was the instrument God had used to make the Cleveland connection. She was so happy. We both rejoiced on the phone and shared about how God had answered our prayers through her and a lady named Linda.

Psalm 37:25 declares, "I was young and now I am old, yet I have never seen the righteous forsaken or their children begging bread." We were now seeing this verse come to fruition in our lives. Robin and I had been Christians for many years and had been through many times where we had to rely on the Lord to provide different things in our lives. We've learned a valuable lesson in this particular scenario. He's never late in answering your prayer. We may think at times He's not listening just because we don't see anything happening on the surface, but God is always at work in our lives even when we don't see it. This one was a real test of patience for me in particular. I had to simply and dependently trust Him. I had no other choice. I was reduced to a raw trust in my God who says he will take care of our needs.

On To Cleveland

Monday came, as did the much anticipated phone call from the hospital scheduler. People don't normally get excited with the prospect of surgery, but on this day I had plenty of enthusiasm.

The plan was to go to Cleveland, meet with the surgeon, go through a battery of pre-operative tests, and undergo surgery to remove the cancer and kidney. All of this would be done in the next five days. As I hung up the phone that day, my mind was now reeling with the details of such a trip and how we would be able to get it all done so quickly. We had two days to be in Cleveland. With so many details, I couldn't imagine how it could all come together. All I know was that the Lord could make a way.

I quickly made airline and hotel arrangements, house coverage and coverage at the church for services. Our lives were on fast forward. And we were not well. Robin was still very much recovering from her surgery just two and half weeks prior, and my energy levels were diminishing. But I knew the Lord had answered our prayers in a huge way, and we had to go. As I now look back on this scenario, I must always remind myself of the provision of God, in that He made a way for us to financially get to Cleveland and cover our expenses before we had ever gotten the initial phone call from Linda. Our sons, daughters-in-law, other family members and friends held a fundraising dinner event in Missouri before we went to Cleveland that helped to cover our expenses. Meanwhile, my volunteer service with the Colorado State Patrol was rewarded with another fundraiser dinner event back in our Colorado town, and our church also planned a fundraiser dinner for us when we returned. God had our expenses totally covered for us before we ever knew what was going to happen. He knew and His love and care for us through so many people was more than we could express. We were, and still are, so grateful for the kindness shown to us during this very trying time in our lives.

We booked a flight for two to Cleveland, Ohio, for that Wednesday. I will never forget how difficult and almost comical it was for us to go through the airports while we were both in wheelchairs. Robin and I could not walk the long corridors of the airports, therefore wheelchair assistance was provided for us. But here we were, the two otherwise young-looking and nearly healthy-looking couple, being wheeled together side-by-side through the airport. It was a sight to behold. At least it looked that way to us, and as we reflect back on this time in our lives, we laugh about it.

We arrived in Cleveland and got checked into our room at the guest house for patients, which was close to the hospital. We were so thankful for this accommodation, but the cost was more than we could pay long-term and moved to another hotel a few blocks away. Thursday would be my appointment with my surgeon, and I would begin the busy schedule of preparing for surgery. As we entered the lobby of this massive facility, we were fascinated with the grandeur of the place. We had never been in such a facility where people from all over the world came to receive care for nearly every malady under the sun. As Robin and I walked down the grand hallways to an elevator, I can remember thinking I was in some type of dream and would perhaps wake up at any moment. Could this truly be happening to us? God had provided a place known to be the number two urological facility in the United States for me? We had no money, no insurance, and here we were! What a phenomenal blessing this was. We stepped on to the elevator and ascended to my doctor's office.

I checked in at the front desk where there were a number of people working behind the desk, receiving patients and giving instructions. I was given the all-too-familiar clipboard with the common paperwork all new patients receive upon entering a new physician's practice for the first time. I was a bit anxious about this visit, so I quickly filled it out and returned it to the receptionist. A few moments went by before my name was called to come to the front desk. I met a male receptionist who asked me to go down to a booth where I would have to talk with a financial counselor.

Oh no. If I can't pay for this, they may not allow me to have the surgery, and then what? Would I have to go back to Colorado and start over?

I was filled with dread as I approached the financial counselor and sat down in front of him. I asked him if Linda worked there, as I would love to meet her and express my gratitude to her for making me feel accepted and cared for. He was quick to tell me she was no longer working there as of Tuesday. This was two days later. He asked me a few questions and asked how I intended to pay for the surgery and hospital stay. I was quick to tell him about how Linda called me last Friday to tell me about this place, and because it was a foundation, they could offer some help that other places may not be able to help with financially. Linda had said they would take care of it all and not to worry. The counselor replied simply, "Ok, we'll take care of it," and had me sign a few papers.

I often reflect on the encounter with Linda. I don't like to "over-spiritualize" occurrences in life, but I believe she was sent by God to personally oversee my situation. I never met her nor did I ever hear from her again. I do know God used a lady named Linda to answer my prayers and cries for help when I needed it most. When I get to heaven, I'm going to find Linda and I'm going to tell her how she made all the difference for me on that Friday afternoon in January 2010. I was the recipient of a great miracle through her kindness.

CHAPTER 9

OUR EVER-PRESENT
HELP IN CLEVELAND

"God is our refuge and strength,
an ever-present help in trouble.
Therefore we will not fear, though the earth give way
and the mountains fall into the heart of the sea,
though its waters roar and foam
and the mountains quake with their surging" (Psalm 46:1-3).

Cleveland was the place where I believe God proved Himself
to be that ever-present God in our lives more than ever before.
Although we had several family members with us to help with
so much (and we are grateful), these were great days of utter
dependence in our God to help us with this new venture. We
were far removed from our home and our surroundings. We
weren't here for vacation or a time of relaxation (especially if
you've ever been to Cleveland in February.) This was a life-
changing event that would literally determine many decisions
for us depending on the surgery I was about to receive in the
coming days.

Psalm 46:1-3 has become one of my favorite and most meaningful scriptures, and I've used this passage in many instances while dealing with others who are going through difficult times. It's a passage of hope and assurance to me that no matter how difficult life becomes or whatever we may be facing, God is an "ever-present" God. The hopeful part of this verse says, *"...we will not fear, though the earth give way and the mountains fall into the heart of the sea, though its waters roar and foam and the mountains quake with their surging."*

I like to interpret it this way: Because God is an ever-present God, we don't have to fear, even if the whole world comes apart and falls into the sea. He's God, and we should not fear what can happen to us even in the face of death. He will help us; He will be there close to us even when we're seemingly on our own in a city far away from home and family while facing a life-altering cancer surgery. Fear is a tool and emotion Satan likes to use to take our attention away from who God is in being ever-present. This scripture has reminded me and reassured me of His omniscience and omnipresence, and He will help me. He will help you, so don't fear, and be assured of His presence in your life on a personal level. He sees you and knows every intricate detail of your life. As you trust Him, allow His presence to overtake whatever fear you may be dealing with, and know He is an ever-present God IN your situation.

My Doctor Appointment

Thursday came in Cleveland. It was the end of January and oh, so cold. We made our way up to my much anticipated doctor's office. After I had a few preliminary tests in the office, we were ushered back to the examination room. It wasn't long before a young man in a white coat entered our room and introduced himself. He asked some questions, examined me, and looked at the records I had brought with me from previous visits and tests in Colorado. As he began to speak, our heads began to be filled with a myriad of details.

He said he could do the surgery to remove my tumor and would do it laparoscopically (using small incisions and lens), which was an astonishing procedure given the size of my tumor. My right kidney and adrenal gland would also have to be removed. I told him my doctor in Colorado didn't know anyone who could attempt the surgery, and he simply assured me this was common for him. He had no problem undertaking my procedure with success. He gave me some options for a surgery date, and I chose the following Monday, February 1. Our minds were reeling as we were thinking about how much had changed in just a few short hours. It was just a few days ago that I was wondering if I would even get the needed surgery, and here we were scheduling it in Cleveland, Ohio. When God is in something, He always makes a way, a BIG way to get it accomplished. The next few days would be testing and more pre-operative testing than I ever knew possible.

One afternoon while I was getting tested, Robin shared with a woman in the waiting room about the goodness of God in our situations and why we were there in Cleveland, and she confessed to Robin that she has strayed from the Lord and needed to get back to serving God. Robin assured her she would be praying for her. We took every opportunity during this time to share about the grace we were so blessed to receive.

The weekend seemed long as I anticipated my surgery to remove the "beast" from my body on Monday morning. Nothing else seemed important to me at the time. I wanted this to be over and all well. Monday morning came, and we arose early to get to the hospital in sub-zero temperatures. As we entered the surgical part of the hospital, the anticipation grew for all of us. Robin was healing and moving slowly from her abdominal surgery. She was doing all she could to be supportive and loving, as she was dealing with her own painful recovery. I checked in, was provided a pager, and told about the procedure as I was in the operating room. Robin, our children and family could watch for my "number" on the visual monitor screen to follow my surgery progression and know when I was out of surgery. We waited in the waiting room for what seemed like days, but it may have only been a short time when my pager went off.

We found ourselves being ushered down a hall and into a surgical preparation area. I remember being somewhat anxious about this procedure, but not fearful. A peace enveloped me that completely overtook my spirit. I was at complete peace with whatever the Lord's will was in these moments. I knew if God had put this all together, He was orchestrating the rest. I was blessed have the care I was receiving in this place, and I knew it would be okay, whatever the outcome. We prayed for the Lord's will and the surgery—I was prepped and ready to go.

In short order, a nurse came through the door, I was given a moment to kiss Robin and my children, and then was wheeled down the long corridor to the awaiting operating room with surgeons and nurses. As they wheeled me down the corridor, I was in awe at the number of operating rooms they had in that place. We stopped outside the room where I would be in just a few minutes and was asked a few questions just to be sure I was the right patient and the procedure. They asked me if I was ready, and I said, "Yes, let's go."

As I entered that sterile, bright operating room, I remember asking the Lord to take it from here. As I think about it now, I'm convinced He had this taken care of long before then. The doctors and nurse helped me get over onto the surgical table, and I was surrounded by professionals who were asking questions and joking with me a bit. Then...

I was in a deep sleep and in the Lord's care. The surgery had begun.

The surgery lasted for what seemed to be just a few minutes, but as I opened my eyes in the recovery room, I was aware it was over. In reality, the surgery lasted for three and a half hours. I could see Robin by my side and talking to me briefly before she was asked to leave. I was again off to sleep. I later learned I was closely being monitored because I had lost quite a bit of blood during the surgery and had to be transfused. The tumor had invaded the inferior vena cava (major artery out of the kidney) to some extent, which is common with large tumors. While the surgeon was working to remove it, I lost the blood.

The following blog entry was written by our daughter, Heather, the day after my surgery in Cleveland.

"One of my favorite scripture verses: "Count it all joy my brothers whenever you face trials of many kinds because you know that the testing of your faith develops perseverance…" At this point our family is sure developing the perseverance. As I sit and watch my dad in a hospital bed and my mom still recovering and in pain, you can't help but dwell on the trials. Then you think about the Lord and how gracious He is and every opportunity He gives us. He has given all of us another wonderful day, as I watch both of my parents, they are living examples of God's love constantly serving their children and each other in any way they can. They use every opportunity, praying with a taxi driver or just holding a door open for someone.

Dad is showing signs of feeling a lot better today, joking around some and getting up and sitting in a chair. He lost quite a bit of blood during surgery, so they ended up giving him a blood transfusion last night. He seems to be doing quite well for his condition, and we praise the Lord for that. Mom is doing so well for having surgery three weeks ago, Rich has been a huge blessing to her I know, just being able to wheel her around the hospital and help in any way.

Jason wasn't able to come to Cleveland but he will be a great help to them in the weeks ahead, as we are spreading out the help they do get so they can have help for several weeks. I am headed back now to Des Moines; what a hard thing to do to leave them, but we know they are in God's hands. We praise the Lord for the strength he continues to give them and give the entire family. Thank you all so much for your prayers and support, we have an even bigger family than we realized. We will keep you updated any chance we get."

Thanking the Lord for our parents,

Heather, Rich and Jason

God Doesn't Make Mistakes

It was one thing for God to provide me with an opportunity to be in Cleveland, but it was quite another to know He even had my room ready for me after the surgery. I am keenly aware of God's providence and care in our lives, but I am also now aware that He makes divine appointments for us even when we are going through difficult times ourselves. We are not islands unto ourselves. We must allow the Lord to direct and use us in whatever state we're in, and I don't mean just a geographical location.

I was wheeled to a semi-private room with a man who had also just had a kidney surgery. His family surrounded him, and over the next few days we developed a relationship with him and his family. I offered to pray for him when all was calm and visiting hours were over. For me, it only seemed like the right thing to do. For him, it was a blessing and touched him deeply. One morning while he was on a call with his mother, I overheard him speaking in a trembling voice and telling her how I prayed for him. Robin and I were able to minister to him and his family during our stay, and we made an impact on their lives in a way that led to phone calls even after our discharge.

My lesson? God always has a plan for us, and that plan reflects His glory *in* all we're going through in spite of *what* we're going through. If we see the opportunity and seize it, He'll put it to good use for His purposes. The things we take for granted as believers like prayer for someone can be a tremendous blessing to the recipient. It's what we should feel privileged to do.

I spent five days in the hospital and was discharged with an appointment to see a medical oncologist on campus. I could not fly for two weeks after surgery, so I had time for follow-up appointments. It was difficult to get around for both of us with Robin recovering from her surgery just a few weeks before mine. In fact, our abdominal surgeries made it almost impossible to use these muscles for even simple tasks, like lying down or rising from bed. The physical challenges rested mainly on our family members, as they would carefully lay us down at night and come in to sit us up in the morning. We were quite the sight. I am so grateful for our children and my siblings for their help to us during this time.

The Oncologist

I checked in for my appointment to see the oncologist and took my place in the waiting room. A few minutes later I was being ushered down a hallway to an examination room where a slim, middle-aged doctor met Robin and me. He spoke with me a few moments about my diagnosis and surgery, and then he began to talk about my treatment options. Simply put, renal cell carcinoma (RCC) was resistant to chemotherapy and radiation, but he offered me a trial medication offered by way of a study program. No guarantees and he told me RCC can be a poor prognosis given the size and scope of my tumor. All things considered, it was not a positive appointment. He suggested I see an oncologist when I returned to Colorado. I thanked him, and we left.

I came away from that encounter not knowing what to think or do. All I knew was that I didn't want this cancer and only hoped it would not spread to other parts of my body. Robin and I prayed and continued to trust God. He was all we had, and He was all we needed! We were still facing the valley before us, but we knew our God was leading the way as he had continued to do up to this point. We had no reason to mistrust Him now.

Faith is not truly faith until it is tried and tested. All of the ingredients of a cake are not considered useful until those ingredients come together and are mixed. Even then it is not a useful product until the heat is applied and it's baked to completion. Then, and only then, will it be considered a cake. So it is with our faith. Exercising our faith and living in it is far different than simply proclaiming faith. Anyone can make a proclamation, but living it out yields results. The result grows fruit that lasts. The fruit lasts eternally and many times cannot be seen with temporal vision. It's the kind of faith that causes us to trust. He is there in every valley and on every mountaintop even when we don't see the result immediately. Our faith equals "trust in the raw," and sometimes we must be reduced to nothing in order for our faith to grow in Him. It's a special place. It's an intimate place to be with the Master as He peacefully sleeps in the bow of the boat while the storm rages around us.

This is where Robin and I were in Cleveland as our time there drew to a close. We were there for nearly three weeks. He had provided for us in tangible and non-tangible ways as we prepared to go from this place, still holding fast to His guiding hands.

We would now prepare to return to Ozark, Missouri, where we would begin the healing process while staying with family friends who had been so generous in opening their home to us. We would always be indebted to these friends for their sacrifice and care for us over the next thirty days in March 2010. It was here in this place that we would be afforded the opportunity to be surrounded by our children and grandchildren during our healing process, which always has a healing effect for close families such as ours.

It was also here in this place as the lead pastor of our church that I would continue to provide leadership from afar and help make decisions. This too was a learning curve for me, as I have always been hands-on while making decisions. The Lord helped me to allow others in leadership to lead, as I had no choice in the matter.

CHAPTER 10

THE BEAUTIFUL BODY

"...so in Christ we, though many, form one body, and each member belongs to all the others" (Romans 12:5).

The body of Christ has always been an amazing organism. From the book of Acts, we see the body in action when persecution came to the Church. We see the body in action when Peter was jailed and people prayed on his behalf. "So Peter was kept in prison, but the church was earnestly praying to God for him" (Acts 12:5). The body of Christ on earth is the one agent whereby we should be able to depend on His hands extended when we find ourselves in a difficult place or valley situation.

I believe it is the Church's responsibility to be a blessing to each other, mandated by the very fact that we are one body in Christ, and we all belong to that same family. We should be a blessing to other family members who are hurting and going through difficult times. We should not differentiate based on color, race, sex, societal status, or any other determinant. The only determining factor should be the common forgiveness and freedom we all come to through the blood of Christ. It's what defines us and identifies us as the body of Christ. We are one body. When the body hurts or one member of the body hurts, we all hurt in some way or another. We have seen this played out on a national and local level when a man or woman of God falls short, and they succumb to sin that hurts us all. Prayer for another member of the body is essential, but is it enough? Sometimes it is, but all too often we simply feel we are "doing our part" by offering up a five-minute prayer.

Prayer is just the tip of the iceberg.

We live in a society that is concerned with the probability of getting too involved if we move beyond prayer. Prayer doesn't cost us much, and we can do it in a few minutes. But when we're called alongside to pay a bill, buy clothing, buy a meal, or even provide a restorative plan for someone who has fallen, then it gets risky. We dig into our resources for someone we may not even know. The body of Christ doesn't act this way. The body of Christ is called upon to get beyond ourselves at all costs for the sake of a brother or sister in Christ. It is putting others first, and it is selfless. It's the same, perfect type of loving sacrifice we see modeled in the loving eyes of Jesus, as He hung between earth and sky and looked out over *all* of humanity with nothing but forgiveness in His plan for all of us who were guilty as charged. It was the ultimate sacrifice once and for all. For far too long, the world system has been doing the job the Church should have been doing in providing for those less fortunate and showing the love of Christ in practical ways.

Robin and I have seen and have been the recipients of the Church's love and generosity, especially in the past several years. After we returned from Missouri to La Junta, Colorado, Robin and I were far from being physically recovered; however, we were getting around well enough to resume our church duties to some extent and begin ministry functions on a limited basis. Our small church and community went into action on our behalf and rallied behind us to support us and love us through this difficult time. Our church congregation took the initiative and held a special fundraiser dinner in the community where more than four hundred people came and showed their support and love. It was simply amazing to see an already economically hard hit town come together for us in our situation. We were humbled and touched beyond belief. We will always be indebted to that loving church and community for their sacrificial giving of time and resources to help us in our hour of need. The following journal entry is from March 10, 2010, after receiving a wonderful outpouring of love from our church and community in Colorado:

"Our church here held a benefit dinner for us on Saturday night, and we were amazed and humbled at the outpouring of love for us. The body of Christ and our community are simply amazing. We have been touched deeply, and we appreciate the support more than can be expressed in words. Our lives have truly been enriched to be part of such a great fellowship and to be blessed with so many great friends who are supporting us in our hour of trials.

Our attitudes will remain positive as we move forward; not knowing what tomorrow will bring to us in a physical way. We have many hurdles to get over yet, but our God goes before us to make a way. The bills have begun to come in from our surgeries, doctor office visits, and all that comes from these types of cancers and treatments. If you've ever had to go to an emergency room for even one visit, you understand how expensive it can be. We are not shaken by what could be an overwhelming mountain before us, but we have laid these things before God to help us for our help comes from Him. Please don't get the impression that we are complaining. It's the reality of what comes when you don't have medical insurance, and we knew we would face these obstacles along with the physical maladies along the way.

The oncologist has already told Robin she cannot have a PET scan because it's too expensive. We rejoice, for Paul said it best in Romans 5:3: "Rejoice in your sufferings, for suffering produces perseverance, perseverance character and character hope." It's easy to worship God when things are going well, but life holds so many uncertainties. Sometimes it comes in the way of suffering. Even in suffering we are to rejoice. We rejoice, because suffering produces qualities we cannot get otherwise. We can only have these things through the power of the Holy Spirit in us to help us. Yes, we are facing some mountains, but we have a relationship with the One who is the mountain mover.

It was great to be back in our church yesterday on a limited basis, and I'll be back in the pulpit on Sunday (03/21). I still have some pain to deal with on a daily basis in my lower abdomen, and Tylenol and Ibuprofen help to alleviate this for me adequately. Robin is still experiencing some discomfort and incision pain periodically, and she takes Tylenol for that. Thank you in advance for your prayers as we both face further doctor follow-up visits and tests. We'll keep you posted.

Friends, we are thankful for you, and pray God's richest blessings for each of you. May the great Mountain Mover move mountains on your behalf this very hour.

With Grateful Hearts,
Rich & Robin"

"Therefore, as we have opportunity, let us do good to all people, especially to those who belong to the family of believers" (Galatians 6:10, NIV).

The body of Christ is beautiful, because the body of Christ should portray the heart and mind of Christ, *especially to those who belong to the family of believers.*

As you read this, may you be inspired and challenged to BE a blessing to someone who needs a kind word, a meal, or help in some form or another. It's one of the great privileges we have in this life in serving the Lord. When we serve others, we serve Jesus. When we serve Jesus, we make a Kingdom difference.

CHAPTER 11

MORE HURDLES IN THE VALLEY

"Do you not know that in a race all the runners run, but only one gets the prize? Run in such a way as to get the prize" (1 Corinthians 9:24, NIV).

Life has hurdles. It's just a plain, unadulterated fact. Some seem to have more hurdles than others, but we all have hurdles. I've never been one to tackle athletic competition. As a young boy, my lack of coordination limited me to serious competitions in nothing but checkers and chess.

I've watched years of Olympics, and the discipline and focus of the athletes never ceases to amaze me, yet only one will come away with a gold medal in any single competition. They all compete and do their very best, but they know when they begin the training process, it's going to be a long arduous and even painful experience. They are willing to take the challenge to go into training and ultimately end up on the world stage in the Olympic Games to compete for the prize. They understand what's at stake. There will major hurdles before them.

In 1 Corinthians 9:24, Paul implores the reader to "run in such a way as to get the prize." Paul is one who understood what running a disciplined race meant. He also knew about hurdles along the way, but hurdles weren't stop signs for him. Hurdles in a race simply mean we have to jump a little higher to clear the obstacle before us, and by faith, we'll have to be prepared for them along the way. The "prize" for the Christian is not a gold medal or a crown made from an olive branch, but the Crown of Life that has been paid for by the blood of Jesus. It's heaven, and He's prepared a place for those who run the race and complete the race with perseverance, focus and discipline in spite of the hurdles life can bring.

As Robin and I returned to Colorado in March 2010, we could not have known what challenges and hurdles lie before us, but we slowly resumed our ministry responsibilities and daily schedules. We remained cognizant of the fact that we had to keep a keen eye on our health situations. Robin would continue to have follow-up appointments with her surgeon and ongoing tests in Pueblo, and I would begin seeing a doctor as well to follow-up on my progress. Our lives were inundated with so much personally now and in every way imaginable. The weight of it all came down on me in a big way as I began to think about all we'd been through in the past couple of years, and I simply began to unravel emotionally. I realized, though that I could not stay there very long. Robin needed my support and so did the church I was leading. The Lord began to deal with my heart as you can read from this journal entry of April 9, 2010:

I repent Lord. Please forgive my attitude and search my heart. Today started out as a day like so many do here in southern Colorado, as a beautiful spring day with warm sunshine settling on us. We began our day early and started our drive to Pueblo as we have done so many times before for—yet another test, (CT scan) of Robin's liver and a dentist appointment to repair Robin's broken tooth, which happened last night while eating dinner. While I was driving, the weight of all that has transpired in the several months began to "settle" on me and take an emotional toll. The questions began to invade my mind and spirit.

"How many more tests? How many more doctor visits? How many more miles? Where will it end? How will it end?"

I don't like seeing my wife stuck with more needles to inject iodine into her system, and see her go through more tests. So many questions; so few answers. Next week, more of the same. As the day wore on and we accomplished our tasks, I carried this weight. All of the weight of the last three months came down around my ears like an ominous storm cloud.

As the day drew close to an end, the Lord began to minister to me as I reread a precious passage of Scripture that has recently become my encouragement and strength. Romans 8:15 from The Message tells me, "This resurrection life is not a timid, grave tending life but an adventurously expectant life that asks 'What's next Papa?'" The passage goes on to tell us how Jesus goes through the hard times and good times with us. In fact, He understands what we go through in mind, body and spirit, and the Spirit of God intercedes on our behalf. The Lord came to my aid by sending a dear friend and fellow pastor to call me and pray with me. What a wonderful God we serve. Even in my whining, He came alongside me with an encouraging phone call and prayer from another state at just the right moment. We all need to be reminded of these precious truths because my guess is that there are other people who go through difficult moments, even on "sunshiny" days. The enemy of our souls would like nothing better than for us to focus on the "things of earth," and in doing so, we fail to see the precious hand of God at work in our lives "in" every situation. So I had to repent of my meltdown and look to the One who has brought us this far. He continues to bless us, keep us and provide for us. He deserves all the praise for His goodness, provision and strength.

Next week, we will return to Pueblo to learn of the results from Robin's scan today, meet with a genetics counselor, an oncologist and a urologist. Another busy week is in store. Would you please pray specifically for good reports, physical and emotional strength and focus on the eternal perspective? Thank you for your continued prayers and support. We love you.

With Heads Lifted High,
Rich & Robin"

The enemy of our souls was working overtime to try to get us to keep our eyes fixed on anything but the race set before us. The Lord was helping us to maintain our focus as we moved forward in our lives. Over the next several months, Robin began seeing an oncologist in Pueblo and I saw a RCC specialist in Denver. Her oncologist wanted to begin treating her with chemotherapy as a precautionary measure, even though there wasn't any evidence from the scans that the cancer was evident in her body. We rejoiced in this fact, but now Robin faced a major decision in whether to be treated with chemotherapy or not. She prayed—we prayed—about this decision and felt that the Lord would guide her to a nutritional approach through dietary means.

Robin has always been a disciplined person, but to watch her eat like no one I'd ever seen was a real testament to her commitment. She was determined to do her best without treatments she knew would only diminish her immune system. I remember sitting in the oncologist's office with her when she told him of her decision to eat better and try a nutritional approach, and he simply balked at the very suggestion, saying there has never been any evidence that diet or nutrition would help cancer. We knew she had made the right decision for her. This would not be the last time she would be faced with having to make this decision along the way.

When I saw my oncologist in Denver for the first time, he ordered a CT scan of my chest abdomen and pelvis which would become the "norm" for me in the months ahead. In the days following the test, my mind was reeling once again with anxiety and questions of whether or not I would have any new cancer growth in my organs, as RCC can oftentimes spread to the lungs, liver, brain and bones. I remember when the call came. There were some small nodules showing on both lungs, but the doctor was reluctant to make a definitive RCC diagnosis as they were so small. His recommendation was to wait and watch them to see if they grew or changed over the course of the next couple of months.

We went through the summer of 2010 continuing to minister and heal physically from our surgeries. We tried not to give much thought to what we were dealing with. We were doing pretty "well" all things considered, and we felt blessed to be able to continue in ministry on a full-time basis. Major decisions had to be made in buying and selling property and moving the church to a transitional place to worship. These things along with the everyday ministry opportunities were keeping us quite busy.

It wasn't long before summer gave way to autumn, and our doctor appointments would continue to be almost routine for us. I would make the three and half hour-drive to Denver and Robin to Pueblo. We would never go without the other. I would jokingly remark about how our "dates" would be spent together at our doctor's appointments and tests. To best describe 2010, it was "The Year" for ongoing tests. CT scans, MRI's, brain scans, bone scans, ultrasounds, and multiple blood draws. Robin continued to show good signs in her labs and tests on a consistent basis. She was feeling stronger as the days turned to months after her last liver surgery, but these were all "hurdles" we had to cross on our journey through this valley.

The summer brought news we had not anticipated hearing from a realtor friend in our town. Our friend told us our (single) landlord had been killed in an accident, thus the house we were living in was in foreclosure proceedings without our knowledge. This left us with the options to stay and wait it out, or find another place to live.

Another hurdle. To make a long story short, the Lord provided once again through some pastor friends who just "happened" to be making a ministry position change in another area of Colorado. The owner of a house (a pastor and great friend) in a neighboring town nearby blessed us by providing us the house for rent. This was a huge hurdle to overcome, but God supplied our need. He also supplied our need in moving by providing extraordinary help from many people in our community and pastor friends. They moved our things in record time.

A Great Gift

I received a call from our daughter-in-law, Tiffany, in August 2010 to inform me of a great blessing. We had not known it, but in September she had nominated Robin to be considered for the James River Assembly's *Designed for Life Woman's Rally* giveaway prize (James River Assembly is an Assemblies of God affiliated church in Missouri). Tiffany was inquiring to see where we would like to go if chosen. I thought about it and decided Hawaii would be a great place we've never seen. I told Tiffany, and she communicated that information to those in Missouri making the decisions. The next thing we knew, we were on a plane and headed to Springfield, Missouri, for the *Designed for Life Women's Rally*. Robin did not know at the time that she had been considered for this blessing, and as far as she knew, James River Assembly was just flying her and me to Springfield to attend the rally.

The day of the giveaway, our whole family except for Robin and Heather were in another room backstage to wait for the presentation. The moment finally came, and Debbie

Lindell called Robin's name to bless her with a prize package to Hawaii. They called our family from behind the scenes which was a surprise for Robin, and I'll never forget the joy, elation, and shock, as we were humbled with this great trip. What could we do? What could we say? We were so blessed by the thoughtfulness and gracious giving by this church. It was a truly highlight of our lives to receive such a blessing. Robin was in utter disbelief as Debbie presented her with the prize package. We wept and embraced each other there in that great sanctuary in Ozark, Missouri, knowing once again: God was walking with us and helping us to be blessed in spite of this long valley we were walking in.

October 2010… Stage IV Cancer

It's never the news you personally want to hear, but this what I was now dealing with as the CT scans were revealing changes in size and shape of the nodules in my lungs. I would now be faced with yet another hurdle I'd have to deal with. Here's my journal entry from October 31, 2010.

"I consider that our present sufferings are not worth comparing with the glory that will be revealed in us" (Romans 8:18, NIV).

I have not updated this site for a while since I waited for the results of my last CT scan. As we drove to Denver last Tuesday to receive whatever report the doctor had for me, Robin and I talked about the possibilities and how we might handle a less-than-favorable report. We had already been down this road several times, and once again, we had to resolve to stand strong in the midst of a possible bad report. God is still God, no matter what happens.

We arrived at the hospital and checked in. We sat in the office for what seemed like years as we waited for the news. The oncologist came in and greeted us. As he pulled up the pictures of my scan, he was not very optimistic. In fact, the results revealed several more nodules on both lungs now, and another nodule (tumor) in my abdomen near my duodenum (stomach exit). This was not what you want to hear, but we had already declared before we arrived that God is still God. This did not take Him by surprise! We were not shocked as we have been in the past by this diagnosis. We wanted to know, "What will we do now?" The doctor told me it was evident now that we were dealing with metastatic cancer, and a clinical trial was in order. We talked about the trial, and he had a coordinator talk to us about it as well. I have decided to start the trial as RCC is resistant to chemo and radiation therapy, and a trial is the only thing we can do, barring a miracle. I will start the trial on November 9; therefore, we covet your prayers for strength and hope in the midst of all of this. I know we face uncertain days ahead, but God is certain and he has a plan even in these trials. Our present sufferings don't even compare to what the Lord is going to do in us. He is giving us the strength, and it's because of your prayers.

We will go to Denver for pre-testing on Monday (11/1) and Tuesday (11/2) to be sure my body will tolerate the trial drugs, so thank you for praying.

Standing Firm in the Trial,
Rich and Robin"

I was presented with a drug study option that day, and we talked about the possible side effects. I was given all of the printed information to read and consider, and we left to go home.

The drive home to southeast Colorado seemed longer than it previously had that day. Although we knew where our hope remained, this was the hurdle I didn't want to cross. I knew metastatic kidney cancer was not a good prognosis, and here we were now facing more physical hurdles. I would be making a decision for treatment in the months ahead, and I was told metastatic RCC is not curable but can be somewhat treatable with newer FDA-approved drugs that can stabilize and/or shrink tumors if one responds well to the treatments.

In the next few weeks, we returned to my Denver oncologist to begin treatment with what is usually a second-line therapy drug used for RCC, but the particular study I was on would require the use of this drug first and then switch over to the first-line drug at some point. I did not know what I was in for as the nurse administered my first dose there in the office, and I drove home from Denver with drugs in hand that day. The drug did not affect me within the first few days, but after approximately six days of this drug, I began to develop mouth ulcers and fatigue that can only be described as unbearable. As I went back to my nurse practitioner for a follow-up in Denver, I remember all too well how she remarked she had never seen such a quick negative response from this drug in anyone before me. I developed nine mouth ulcers inside my mouth and down my throat over time, impairing my ability to eat. The doctor prescribed a special mouthwash that numbed the inside of my mouth in order for me to eat. Is this what I had to look forward to? It was decided by mutual consent and prayer that I would discontinue this drug as soon as possible and switch to the first-line drug as soon as I could recover.

It took nearly two months for me to recover from what was a difficult drug, and the physical toll it was taking on me was draining every ounce of energy. I continued to fight through this valley, continued to preach, and continued to do all of the vocational responsibilities of ministry on a daily basis. It was getting more difficult by the day to continue on with the rigorous ministry schedule, and it was becoming apparent to Robin and me that perhaps a change was in the wind. We began to pray about what direction we should go, knowing I would be transitioning to another drug.

The following journal entry is the last entry of December 28, which will give you a clearer picture of what 2010 in summary looked like for us.

"In just a few days we will begin a new year and a new decade. As I look back at this year and the past several years, I am in awe at the enormity of God's provision and blessing in our lives. I don't know what the future holds; but I am not fearful at all, for as the late Ira Stanphill wrote so long ago, "Many things about tomorrow I don't seem to understand, but I know who holds tomorrow, and I know who holds my hand." I used to fear cancer. I don't anymore. In fact, I've learned to live "in the moment" and enjoy the simple things in life and love my Lord more intimately every day. I suppose dealing with cancers as

Robin and I have is certainly the reason I feel this way, but I'm thankful for that. I take nothing for granted, and expect nothing. Why couldn't I have learned that twenty-five years ago?

I am currently in a holding pattern concerning my medication. I will resume the Afinitor on January 4 on a half dose every other day cycle to see how I tolerate it. Having to deal with lasting side effects from the Afinitor has not been easy. I've been experiencing mouth pain ever since I stopped the meds two weeks ago. My gums are receding in several places exposing the nerves in two of my teeth, and this makes it quite difficult to eat or drink without pain. I'm going to address this issue when I go back to Denver for my next visit on January 3. I am still dealing with the fatigue, but it's not near as bad as when I'm on the Afinitor.

We had a wonderful Christmas here in Colorado with our son-in-law and daughter making a last minute decision to come and spend a couple of days with us. We were truly blessed and wanted to keep them here. I'm sure their bosses would not have appreciated that. It was so nice to enjoy this Christmas and be thankful to the Lord we had another Christmas to celebrate.

Robin and I want to personally thank all of you for your prayers, kind words and gifts to us throughout 2010. We are keenly aware that we are here because of your faithfulness and sacrificial prayer time on our behalf. For that, we are most grateful and humbled. We love you, and pray God's very best for you and yours in 2011.

Nothing will happen in 2011 that God cannot handle.

With Grateful Hearts!

Rich and Robin

We continued on, ending 2010 with uncertainties but being blessed by all God had brought us through. We were blessed to still be here in spite of the hurdles we were facing, but God was lifting us over those hurdles when were too weak to continue. As we looked back at 2010, our hearts were filled to overflowing. We were keenly aware of the blessings our God bestowed on our lives in the midst of great physical trial. He was our Rock throughout the year and brought us through in triumphant praise.

CHAPTER 12

2011...THE YEAR FOR CHANGE

"Every good and perfect gift is from above, coming
down from the Father of the heavenly lights, who
does not change like shifting shadows"
(James 1:17, NIV).

Change is a difficult word to embrace. People generally don't like change, especially in large doses. We like patterns and routines. Get up at a certain time in the morning, eat at a certain time, and heaven forbid someone should sit in "our" seat in church. We are creatures of habit. Robin, our children and I have endured years of change throughout our interstate moves and ministry changes. Starting over: new schools, new friends, new homes. It never seems to get any easier; in fact, it gets more difficult with age.

We did not know what 2011 would present to us, but we did know that although our lives were changing nearly on a daily basis, our hope was in a God who does not change. His character attributes and every good gift had not changed in our seemingly chaotic and ever-changing world. The ongoing doctor visits, physical changes, drug challenges, financial challenges, roller coaster emotions, and all the rest were facing us on a daily basis. January 3 would be my last follow-up appointment in Denver before going on our Hawaii trip. It was determined that I should try a half dose of the drug to see if that would help diminish the side effects I was dealing with.

While in the midst of all the changes, we were unaware of what 2011 would hold for us physically, so we started 2011 by taking advantage of our Hawaii trip in early January. We had an amazing week of rest and mental stress relief, as we were blessed to be in Hawaii. This was certainly a "good gift from above," as we enjoyed each other and the blessing of God's creation.

Here is our post-Hawaii journal entry from January 14, 2011:

It has been too long since my last update, as we have had an extraordinary couple of weeks. Our work and year-end responsibilities and an awesome week in Maui, Hawaii, have kept us more than a little busy. Yes, a week in Maui. This trip was a very special gift from the JRA Women's Ministry back in Missouri, and we were so blessed by their generosity. Our daughter-in-law, Tiffany, nominated Robin to receive a special gift package back in August of last year, and she was chosen from one of many nominations. We were given until June of '11 to use the trip and decided to go sooner rather than later. We just returned from Maui, and what a wonderful time we had. Many thanks to Tiffany and the JRA team for making it all possible. We are truly blessed.

We arrived back in Colorado to go to a follow-up doctor appointment on Wednesday to check my blood counts and discuss other possibilities.

While in Hawaii, I stopped taking the Afinitor due to what I thought were side effects from the meds. We still don't know what was causing the severe stomach and abdominal pain I was experiencing, but I am scheduled for another CT scan and bone scan on January 25 to see if I have disease progression or not. If I have disease progression, the plan is to crossover to Sutent, and I have been informed that the side effects from this medication most often are pretty harsh on most patients. My nurse practitioner told me she never saw a patient so adversely affected by Afinitor as me. But everyone reacts differently, and I may respond better on Sutent. We just won't know until we try. I am feeling pretty well generally, but still deal with night sweats, fatigue, and lack of appetite, and my sleep patterns are anything but consistent. It's difficult for me to sleep more than four to five hours in any given night without waking and staying awake.

Robin is currently battling a sinus infection and cough that just won't go away and is on anti-biotics to help combat her illness. She continues to do well from an overall standpoint. We are thankful for that. She strayed from her diet while we were in Maui, but has now resumed. How could anyone go to Hawaii and not take advantage of the delectable delights at every turn?.

We are happy to be back home now, and we will continue to keep you posted on any further developments on the health front. Thank you for your continued prayers and words of encouragement. May 2011 be a blessed year for all of you.

Moving Forward,
Rich and Robin"

As the days turned into weeks, my body would not tolerate the prescribed drug, even at a half dose. My doctor and I determined that I should discontinue its use, take a break, and then switch to Sutent, which is usually the first-line therapy drug for RCC. My body slowly recovered from the side effects of the first drug in the upcoming weeks, and it was so good to begin the healing process in my mouth and other areas.

February was a month which brought about the drug switch that would hopefully bring stability to tumor growth and lessen side effects to me. I'll never forget my first dose of Sutent, which was administered in the oncologist's office. As I held these capsules in my hand, I silently prayed before taking them that God would help me through these new drugs. I would now begin taking four capsules per day, and we would have to wait to see what effect it would have on my body and the cancer.

The next few months would be filled with busyness in ministry and continued follow-up doctor visits to monitor how I was tolerating this new drug. It took several weeks for my body to begin to adjust to this new drug, but when it did, I knew I was need of the Lord's help and strength. This was not good. I began to get extremely fatigued and developed gastrointestinal symptoms, hand and foot syndrome, nose bleeds, and other minor side effects which simply diminished my ability to function without great stress. My sleep patterns were disrupted to a point of only being able to sleep for a few hours at a time. Having said this, we were not complaining and continued to serve the Lord and our congregation in the midst of this battle. Sutent was a drug I would take for a twenty-eight-day period and then take a two week break or "washout period". I looked forward to the break, but it would take the whole two weeks to feel somewhat better before entering into another twenty-eight day regimen.

Meanwhile, Robin continued to enjoy what seemed to be a cancer-free period during these months, and she was a wonderful support and help to me personally and in ministry. I will be eternally grateful for her support and love during a most difficult and trying time for me. On one Sunday morning before church, we were just preparing to leave our driveway when a side effect from the drug caused me to become nauseous. As I was around the side of the house bent over, Robin simply came to my side, placed her hand on my back, and began to rub my back and pray. I was heaving; she was praying. She stood by my side even when it was ugly.

As the next few months came into view and the spring 2011 became imminent, the side effects were beginning to have a far bigger effect on my abilities to continue in a full-time position at the church than I anticipated. We sought the Lord and made a very difficult decision. The first two weeks of April were so physically taxing on me that I could not preach due to severe fatigue and the inability to be cognitively aware of what was going on around me. The bigger issue for me was not about us at all. My primary concern was for the church God had called us and the other ministries we were so deeply involved in here in this rural, Colorado town. The church had been on this physical and emotional journey with us during the past four years, and it was apparent to us that they needed a healthy pastor now who could lead them into new opportunities. The church simply needed to move forward, and we couldn't go with them.

We prayed together, and we made the hard decision to resign our position there and move back to Missouri to be closer to our children and grandchildren. I met with our advisory board and district superintendent, Don Steiger, to inform them of our resignation. They were so gracious to us to allow us to be a vital part in helping make the pastoral change as smoothly as possible in the coming weeks. They allowed us to be directly involved in helping to review resumes and choose a new pastor to come in our absence.

The spring of 2011 was extremely busy as we anticipated our move back to Missouri and began to pack a house for the second time in nine months to make a long drive. Meanwhile, our children were helping us to make the transition as smoothly as possible in Missouri by looking for housing for us and supporting us in every way. They were excited by the fact that we were coming "home."

May came and went, and June was an extremely busy month for us as we were prepared to make our big move to Missouri. Our son, Jason, took some time off from his job to commit a few days to coming to Colorado to help us pack the moving truck and drive the truck back to Missouri. The La Junta Fire Department and other friends in ministry came on moving day and blessed us by packing our truck. We will always be extremely grateful to these friends who so unselfishly and sacrificially gave of their time to help us. We remain friends with these great people God put in our lives to this day!

Moving Day...

We won't forget the day we left southeast Colorado to move back to Missouri. God was our source and strength during some of the most difficult days we had ever faced in ministry and our lives in general. He was our great provider when we wondered if we would face another day or how the bills would get paid. These were just some of the many thoughts that flooded our minds as we headed east out of La Junta, Colorado, toward Springfield, Missouri. When we left, we did not know if we would ever see those folks again this side of heaven. It was a very emotional day as Robin and I, along with our little dog Sammy and our son Jason left that town in mid-June 2011. Tears filled our eyes as we drove east and tried to contemplate all God had done in our lives over the past four years there.

We "grew up" in southeast Colorado. God helped us to grow and mature in the faith there. The lessons He taught us while in the midst of great trial are far more than this book can contain. A few prominent blessings stand out now in hindsight: (1) He showed us over and over again in those days that He is faithful, trustworthy, and true; (2) He never, ever failed us, no matter how difficult or deep the valley seemed, and (3) He was always there to help us through our hard times. We cannot not know the depth of His provision or help until we look back at a certain situation to see just how God brought us through it. Maybe we'll never fully understand this side of heaven, but one thing is for certain. He's faithful to the end. He didn't give up on us while making his way to Calvary, and He's not giving up on us now.

This was our final journal entry while in Colorado from June 2, 2011:

Robin and I have been sharing almost daily about the goodness of the Lord as we reflect on the past four years of ministry here in Colorado. Our time here is nearly coming to a close, and as we have considered the blessings we have received in coming here, it's nearly overwhelming. He has put some wonderful people in our lives in this place, and we are truly going to miss all of you here in La Junta and Colorado who have prayed for us, supported us, and came alongside us to help in the work of ministry.

It's become more apparent to me than at any other time in my life that it's all about people. Jesus died for people, and it's a high honor to be able to minister to people from all walks of life. We've been able to see the transforming work of the Spirit of God at work in the lives of people, and what a remarkable blessing to be a part of that. But the fact of the matter is: I think we have been the recipients who have been given far more than we could ever give back by just serving the Lord and people. Thank you for allowing us to be a part of your lives.

It's been a busy whirlwind of packing, making arrangements on the Missouri side, wrapping up here in Colorado, dealing with ongoing side effects, and trying to find a new physician in Missouri who can treat RCC. It's been tiring and trying to say the least. The real challenge has been trying to find a doctor who will work with me not having insurance. I've just finished my third cycle of Sutent on Monday (5/29), and now I may not be able to continue the treatments without a doctor. I was at these crossroads once before, and the Lord provided for me (and Robin), and we'll trust Him to do it again. It just makes one weary in having to basically start from the beginning again in our quest for new doctors.

I had my last Denver doctor visit on Wednesday (6/1). The usual blood draws and an echocardiogram were in order. My red and white blood cell counts were a little low, as were my platelets, but my nurse practitioner called me today to reveal the results of the echo and cholesterol count. The left ventricle wall of my heart has thickened and my cholesterol is high. She is more concerned about my cholesterol than anything right now and says RCC and high cholesterol don't work well together; in fact, it could be a problem, so she is advising me to take cholesterol medication or try a natural approach. The thickened wall of my heart should not be a problem with controlled blood pressure. We also discussed the pain I'm experiencing on a constant basis in my side and back, and she feels it is very likely the cancer has found its way to my right side rib area. "Something" did show on the last bone scan in that area, and now it protrudes a bit. It was not determined on the scan because it was small then. And so I take daily pain meds to help manage the pain. I'm taking way too many pills now. I'm beginning to feel like a living, breathing Pharmaceutical company. At any rate, I have been contemplating not staying on the treatments anyway, as the side effects are not pleasant.

And so, as we get ready now to move, would you pray for safety as we travel the 600-plus-mile trek back to Missouri? In addition, pray for the Lord to open new doors for us with doctors. We deeply appreciate and covet your prayers.

I am going to try to stay involved in ministry on a limited basis while back in Missouri. God has blessed us with far too much to just sit idly by and not share His goodness when so many need to be encouraged.

Look What The Lord Has Done!

Rich and Robin

The long road into and across Kansas has never shortened. We were now destined and on our way back to Missouri. Robin drove our car while Jason, our dog Sammy, and I sat in the moving truck loaded with everything we owned. We didn't want to look back. Our hearts were torn leaving La Junta that day. Tears filled my eyes as we drove away from the place God had called us to four years prior. He did so much in our lives there, and now due to physical trial, we had to leave. It didn't seem fair; it was not our choice, but only God knew the season we would be there, and now a new day was dawning before us. Our hearts were still in Colorado, but we knew God was leading now through a new, unknown part of the valley, where we would continue to grow and trust Him in the days ahead.

CHAPTER 13

FROM THE COLORADO VALLEY TO THE MISSOURI VALLEY

"Whatever you have learned or received or heard from me, or seen in me—put it into practice. And the God of peace will be with you"
(Philippians 4:9, NIV).

The Apostle Paul was a man of great example in life and deed. It was never about him but all about the message of Christ he portrayed in practical and verbal ways. Because of his testimony, he knew he could confidently instruct others to follow his lead in life and doctrine. He spoke from a Philippian jail cell, and he knew of this "God of Peace" from which he spoke. Even in the midst of his own trials, he instructed others to depend on God as he had. He did not waver in spite of geographical location or circumstances surrounding him.

Robin and I knew we would be facing new challenges in Missouri with having to choose new doctors and the overall challenges associated with a long move. The move went fairly smoothly from Colorado to Missouri. We had a few cosmetic details to complete in our new home, but overall it was a good move. We were happy to be closer to our family and Missouri friends. Those were emotionally difficult days, getting reacquainted with the area, friends, and working through the separation we felt now from our departure in Colorado. We hadn't left Colorado because we were distraught or burned out. We didn't resign under outside pressure. We weren't forced to move, but we knew we must. Our hearts were still there as we tried to make the Missouri adjustment. But we knew the peace of God was there to uphold us and help us make the adjustments.

Our journal entry from July 8, 2011 entitled, "Changing Times":

Coming to Missouri has been and is a barrage of changes for us since coming here nearly a month ago now. Not only have we made some changes to our home, but I now have grass (green grass.) to mow and so many other changes. Our lives have literally taken on a whole new direction. The changes have been good for the most part, but change demands adjustment to reality. I say this because the reality of my disease has become more apparent in the past few days. The fatigue and pain I have been experiencing are stark reminders of what I'm dealing with is not a temporary illness, but one that will get increasingly worse with each passing day. This is reality, but I'm a realist. I know what I'm dealing with and don't want any surprises. None of us are going to live forever on this earth, and that only serves to remind us of the eternity we all face and the importance of finishing well. Finishing well is not about material possessions or popularity but all about the rich deposits we've made for the Lord Jesus Christ while here. Those are the "things" that will not rust or fade away and will be rewarded.

I have taken the advice of my good friend, Dr. Blessman, and have contacted a hospice care provider to summon their help in the days ahead with pain meds, etc. They have come to our home and met with us to discuss their services as needed, and I'm so glad we did. So many people wait until the final days to call on Hospice, and they have so much to offer in other ways. I'm not sure I'll be able to continue on Sutent, as I'm not currently on a study, and it would cost me nearly $9,000 per month if I had to buy it. I have applied for a program through a pharmaceutical company that may be able to help us, but if they don't, I will not be able to continue on the treatments. I should know something next week. I am continuing to wait to hear from a Springfield oncologist for my future scans, labs, and follow-up.

Robin has been continuing to get us settled in our home and has been feeling pretty well. She recently stepped on a staple and punctured her foot which warranted a visit to the clinic for a tetanus shot. Other than that, she's doing well.

We will keep you posted in our progression and other news as it arises in our lives. We appreciate your continued prayers and support, for we are aware how important your prayers are on our behalf.

Changing With The Times!

Rich and Robin

Even in the midst of all the changes, we were experiencing the peace of God, and that's an important part of being in the will of God. Life can swirl at times, but if we follow the path of peace, God won't seem distant when everything else in our lives is seemingly in a state of chaos.

Making the move back to Missouri was on every account a very difficult time for us emotionally, financially, and spiritually. In fact, the months that followed our move were very difficult days for us, as we adjusted to a life we didn't really want to come back to. Oh, we loved our families, friends, and had a great support team in place when we returned, but we had left behind a vision, a people, friends, and a community God called us to minister to in so many ways. We simply delighted in serving as ministers by vocation but even more so by the call of God on our lives.

For the first six months of what I call post-move-reentry, I went through a very difficult time trying to find out where I might "fit in" again. I went through a grieving process as I went from a sense of being needed and appreciated to a life of utter solitude. The questions began to invade my mind: "Will you ever be used in ministering to people again? What will I do now? How will we make it financially? Is life as we know it all over? What's next for us?" The feelings were real, and an ominous cloud began to settle in on me as I contemplated these realities that faced us. It was everything all at once, and now that I had time on my hands, it didn't seem to get better. Did we come back to Missouri to die?

Decision Time

The year 2012 came as any other year does, except something took place in our lives that had a profound impact on how we would respond to the preceding months of doubt and selfish thinking. As we prayed and pushed through the thoughts and emotions, the Spirit of God revealed to us that He would use us in different areas of ministry if we would step out and allow Him to open doors. We made a choice to get up, brush ourselves off, and get out of the "pit," if you will. We were determined to move forward for His honor and glory. We presented to Him where we were now and what we had to offer Him, and God opened up doors of opportunity for us to be more involved in areas of service. We were invited to lead a small life group at our church. We accepted the role with humility and were gracious for the invitation. It wasn't long before our lives slowly came back into focus, as we realized life is not all about us but all about the people God puts in our lives.

We must have spiritual eyes to see the needs and be willing to help where we can with a kind word, prayer, counsel, or whatever God does in the moment. The most important aspect of the Christian life to realize is that God will use what we have to offer Him if we yield it to Him, and it doesn't matter if we're credentialed or not. Societal status doesn't matter. A perfect personality is not a prerequisite for being used by the Lord in His service. In fact, from numerous examples in Scripture, we see quite the contrary being true. It is God who uses whomever He pleases. It comes down to having faith that God can and will use what we have to offer, no matter how insignificant we think it may be. We must be obedient and walk humbly before God, for only He knows the condition of the human heart.

As we have come to learn these truths and put them into practice, God has done more through our cancers than we could ever have done to reach people otherwise. As we stepped out in faith, we made a decision to go to different churches and tell our testimony, encouraging others through what we were dealing with. It wasn't long before we discovered our story and encouragement from Scripture resounded in the hearts of many, many people wherever we went. And as long as God would allow our health to stand strong, we would take a message of hope wherever we were invited. I am convinced that the best remedy for depression is to reach out to others and allow God to use what we have to encourage and minister to those around us. It's impossible to see beyond ourselves when all we can focus on is our situation.

Remember: life is short. Eternity is without end, and Christ's followers have a mandate to take as many with us to heaven as we can. This life is not about us, but all about the One who gave us life.

The Physical Battle Continues

As we continued to believe God for every need, 2012 opened with new opportunities for us. We still faced physical battles and did not know what the months ahead or the new year would hold for us. Robin began to experience yet again some abdominal pain which prompted more blood draws and a PET scan in February 2012. Her rising CEA (cancer markers) and the scan revealed what appeared to be more metastatic cancer in her liver. This was not what we wanted to hear, but once again she was faced with more decisions. After conferring with our local oncologist, it was determined that she would best be served if we consulted with an oncologist and liver specialist in St. Louis at the notable Barnes-Jewish Hospital.

We made the appointment and drove to St. Louis to confer with these doctors with confidence that whatever the problem, they would surely help put this cancer behind Robin and move on. As we met with a very confident surgeon in the hospital, we were filled with assurance that a liver resection could be performed. But it would not be without yielding perhaps eighty percent of Robin's liver. The surgeon assured us he had done this type of surgery in the past, and people do fine post-surgery. We also conferred with the oncologist there, which advised and recommended Robin to have chemotherapy treatments after the surgery. That was something Robin wanted to pray about.

Once again, we were faced with more decisions and not-so-good news, but we were hopeful that God would help us through this ongoing valley of physical issues.

We returned to Springfield and prepared to face another surgery on March 20, 2012. We informed our families of another surgery and informed our pastoral care pastor at our church. We were as prepared as anyone could be for surgery; in fact, we were all but too used to this procedure. People were praying and lifting our names before God in anticipation of this surgery.

Robin and I drove to St. Louis on March 19, which was our thirtieth anniversary. This was not how we envisioned celebrating this milestone anniversary, but we don't get to pick and choose how these things go. We were just happy to be celebrating the day we weren't sure we would celebrate a few years earlier. We stayed with some wonderful friends on the Illinois side when we arrived in St. Louis, which made the commute and financial situation for lodging so much easier for our family. We will be forever thankful to Tom and Lana for being such great friends in our hour of need.

We awoke early on March 20 with anticipation in our hearts as we faced yet another surgery, but this one would be the most comprehensive in leaving behind a large portion of Robin's liver. We drove over to St. Louis that morning as prepared as you can ever be for such a surgery, but we prayed and felt strongly that God had it still under control, no matter what.

Robin checked in, she prepped, and our pastoral care pastor (Mark) was there to pray and encourage us before Robin went into surgery. It wasn't long, and the nurse came to wheel her into the operating room while we exited to the surgery waiting area for any news during the surgical procedure. The surgery was expected to last three to four hours, depending on how it went for them and how well Robin did.

We were in the waiting area approximately one and a half hours when I was paged to come to the surgical consultation room to meet with the surgeon. My mind began to race. "What could it be?" I asked myself. Perhaps she did better than they anticipated? I didn't want to think the worst, but I knew in my heart it was either very good news or very bad news. A surgeon who is working on your wife does not come out of the operating room just an hour and a half after beginning a major surgical procedure. I braced myself, took in a deep breath and rallied the family in the consult room as we waited for the doctor to come in.

He was resolute and spoke calmly as he told us his predicament in layman's terms. He could not see on a scan what he had found in Robin's liver until he had actually opened her up. Once he started the operation, he realized that the cancerous tumor was impinging on her portal vein (a major vein carrying large amounts of blood) in the liver. It would be too risky to try to resect it. He also saw that there appeared to be some swollen lymph nodal involvement. These two factors helped us make a decision to abort the surgery entirely and close her up. I asked the hard questions, breaking the momentary silence.

"Doctor, what's the best-case scenario and worst-case scenario for Robin?"

He was quick to respond. Best-case was that with a positive treatment response, she could survive perhaps two to two and a half years. Without treatment, she may have a year or a little less. He went on to talk about the new chemo drugs and treatments; we thanked him and exited the room. Our family was somewhat stunned as we looked at each other early that morning. As I had done so many other times with families, I tried to bring some comfort with words. But the fact of the matter was I was now trying to console myself as well as my family with this latest news. We were all contemplating what we had just heard. How would I break this news to Robin? She went into the surgery feeling like they were going to remove this cancer, and now it would be just the opposite result. She had been cut, but nothing happened to resolve the issue. This was stunning, to say the least.

I felt like I was reliving my mother's surgical procedure in Boston, Massachusetts, when I was fifteen. Mom had liver cancer, and the prognosis was very similar, in that the cancer had invaded the common bile duct and all that could be done was to place a bypass tube in her liver around the bile duct to divert the bile from the cancerous area. I will never forget that sense of utter dependence on God in that moment when the doctor said, "We've done all we can do." God is the only one at that moment who can do anything, but it's still a feeling of "hitting the wall" and leaving us with a human sense of shock and vulnerability. It's just the way we're made, but we must not stay in that state. I believe Satan can and will try to take full advantage of these vulnerable moments and cause us to doubt God or plague our minds with questions that perhaps cannot be answered here on earth. It's in these moments when many people begin to doubt God's existence and ability. These are decision-making moments for the Christ follower, and we must not linger long but simply take God at His word by faith. He is who He says He is and can do what He says He can do. In an hour when we need Him most, He'll be there to comfort and supply our needs.

I've known far too many when faced with seemingly impossible odds just become bitter at God and never recover. It doesn't have to be that way. This was not an option for Robin and me as we faced these valley experiences in our lives. With all good or seemingly difficult news, we left it in His hands. We trusted our Lord with our lives. He's our Creator, and He alone knows the outcome. Our bodies will fail, but the soul will never die, therefore it makes far more sense to keep that in excellent shape for eternity. Keeping your soul healthy begins by exercising our faith, trust, and relationship with Him. No matter what happens here, we must be prepared for eternity.

We did not tell Robin the surgical outcome until she recovered enough to contemplate what we were telling her, so it was a day or two after the surgery when I broke the news to her. Her initial reaction was disappointment. She was just disappointed at the whole situation and that she had to endure a surgical procedure with no results. It was a sobering thought for both of us to come to a world-renowned hospital with high expectations and go home post-surgery the same way she came in, except for an incision. It took a few days of prayer, talking it out, and acceptance to process it all.

In the days that followed her surgery, Robin was now faced with a decision of whether or not to begin chemotherapy treatments. Several doctors came in to discuss it with her, and ultimately she made a decision to not accept chemotherapy as an option but chose quality versus quantity as her final decision. Her surgeon came in to discuss the surgery result with Robin, and he gave her his prognosis of about one year with no chemotherapy, based on his findings.

She simply stated, "I serve a big God. Man has done what he can do, BUT God. Now, it's His turn." He didn't know how to respond to that statement, but he did say, "Let me know how it goes with you. Keep me informed." Looking back, she has never regretted her decision to not move forward with chemotherapy, as it has afforded her multiple opportunities to spend quality time with family and friends and to be able to do the things she's wanted to do without being physically impaired.

Robin was discharged several days later with post-surgical follow-up instructions, and we returned to Springfield to begin her healing process. The months that ensued were filled with all the busyness and the ministry opportunities we could physically endure. I began working with Convoy of Hope on a volunteer basis, helping to train and lead church volunteers across the nation in select outreaches on how to lead and disciple others to Christ. We prayed for people in the Prayer Tents at outreaches. Robin and I also traveled, preached and testified in different churches where we had the opportunity throughout the year.

In the latter part of 2012, Robin began developing some new symptoms for which we had to see a gastroenterologist. Earlier that year (March), we were told by her surgeon in St. Louis after the surgery that she would begin to see certain symptoms develop, and time would prove this to be true. After having a few tests, it was determined that the tumor(s) were beginning to press against the bile ducts and alter the flow of bile from her liver, thereby causing bile to backup in her liver and cause problems. If something couldn't be done, jaundice and itching would ensue. We met with the specialist who suggested a stent be placed in the bile duct to avert the symptoms and allow the bile to flow more freely from her liver. We were planning on traveling to Pennsylvania for Thanksgiving, and the doctor suggested the procedure be performed before going there.

The week before Thanksgiving, Robin went in for the outpatient procedure to place a stent high in the bile duct of her liver which was nearly closed. The bile began to flow immediately, and we were grateful for this procedure. The procedure would have repeated in 3 months, as the stent began to clog up. She was discharged and told to watch out for symptoms of pancreatitis, and within twenty-four hours, pancreatitis began to develop with pain coursing through her side and back. She was admitted to the hospital for the weekend. Within a day, the symptoms began to subside and she was discharged. Needless to say, the doctor advised us we could travel, and we were on our way to Pennsylvania that following day to spend quality time with family and friends for Thanksgiving. We had an awesome time visiting, ministering in different churches and spending precious time with loved ones.

For me, the RCC has steadily and persistently progressed in my lungs. A CT scan in the fall of 2012 revealed a lung nodule which had more than doubled in size since that summer, and fatigue is still a constant battle for me. But we continue to trust God and believe Him for our healing here in this life or in eternity. We win either way!

CHAPTER 14

THE VALLEY OF THE SHADOW OF DEATH

"Even though I walk through the darkest valley, I will fear no evil,
for you are with me; your rod and your staff, they comfort me"
(Psalm 23:4, NIV).

I've always feared deep water. I grew up on the Delaware River which borders New Jersey and Pennsylvania. In some places, the river grew wide and dropped down to immensely deep levels. I loved to fish this river when I had the opportunity, but I hated peering into the unknown, dark water. Many people over the years had lost their lives here because of undercurrents and the sheer inability to know what was beneath them. I couldn't see what was there and I never wanted to test it.

As we entered 2013, we began the new year with the same anticipation of good things to come but we had no idea what lie in store for us physically and otherwise. We knew the diagnosis of the surgeon in St. Louis, and that was nearly a year ago. Robin had a stent placed in her liver at the end of 2012, but what could we expect in the coming days and months? Would

God miraculously heal us both in this life, or would we face uncertain physical trials in the days ahead? This was a deep place that we could not see with our human eyes, but we had to trust God to lead us.

About midway through January 2013, Robin began to develop a fever and an overall feeling of flu-like symptoms. A persistent cough developed, and her strength waned on a daily basis. Our doctor suspected a virus, and we were told it would have to run its course and were sent home with instructions. I treated her with the usual fever reducing medicines, gave her plenty of fluids and fed her as she felt the need to eat.

This continued for several weeks with persistent fevers, coughs and violent shaking spells. Robin would lie in her bed and cry out in a loud voice to the Lord for relief, and I would stand beside her, pray for her and tried to console her. It was a scene that tore at my very core as I stood next to her, trying to help in any way I could. I was concerned about her physical ability to be able to fight whatever was ravaging he body, and I found it difficult to sleep at night for fear I would find her not breathing. I would wake up and place my hand on her to make sure she was breathing. One evening, I was awakened to such violent shaking in her body that she literally shook me awake. The next morning, I called our doctor to explain what was happening, and he admitted her to the hospital that day. Blood culture tests and other tests were conducted in the next day or so, only to reveal a blood infection. The doctor told Robin he was surprised she had survived as she did with this infection in her body at home. This was startling news to us.

We had no idea we had just come through the valley of the shadow of death.

She was admitted for a period of six days where it was discovered that the stent in her liver was completely blocked by bile, thus causing the infection in her blood. Intravenous antibiotics were administered, and another stenting procedure was performed to alleviate the symptoms and get the bile flowing once again. The doctor was shocked to find the stent blocked after being there just ten weeks, as it wasn't due to be changed until twelve weeks had passed. He informed us that he would schedule it to be changed in ten weeks the next time. Robin's fever subsided, and her appetite began to come back. She was given a prescription maintenance regimen of antibiotics and pain medicine to go home with and discharged on February 4, 2013.

My New Valley...

I began to develop symptoms nearly a year and a half ago in my lower digestive tract that had me concerned enough to bring it to my oncologist's attention. Nothing was ever pursued, and life went on as usual. I felt as if I should have the normal 50-year-old colonoscopy at some point, but I thought it might be a moot point, since I already had cancerous nodules in both lungs. But in January 2013, I began to develop more concerning symptoms which prompted me to pursue a colonoscopy. I called the gastroenterologist that did Robin's recent procedures and made and appointment for a consultation. It was decided that I should have the procedure. I was concerned about what the doctor would find given the nature of my symptoms, and we scheduled it for mid-January.

The appointed day came, and I was wheeled down another corridor to another awaiting procedure room. It was all too familiar. I was given a lighter dose of sedation and the procedure began. I was awake and coherent for the duration of this procedure as the doctor examined my colon. He came to a place where he stopped, and as I looked at the scene before me on the screen, it was a picture of something I had seen in Robin's first colonoscopy in 2007. The ugliness of what I was viewing was all too familiar. It was a tumor in my transverse colon. He confirmed what we were both seeing and took several biopsies. He told me we'd have a pathology report in a couple of days to see if it was a new primary colon cancer or a metastatic renal cell tumor. I was not shocked but more disappointed at the fact that I had yet another tumor inside my body to somehow deal with.

In the days that followed, the report came back that I was more than likely dealing with RCC in my colon and would have to make a decision of how to deal with it. It would cause me great difficulties in the days and weeks ahead. My oncologist suggested a surgical approach to the newly-found tumor, but this was a thought I was not too keen on, as recovery would be long and limited for me, and would ultimately not heal the underlying problem. I would also be forced to not be able to help Robin in the days ahead, as she will need help.

The next few months now will be challenging in the physical sense, and we may walk through the valley of the shadow of death, but we're also reminded of the fact that we don't have to fear, because His rod and staff comfort us.

CHAPTER 15

PEACE IN THE MIDST OF THE STORM

*The following chapter was written by Robin Johnson, who wanted the reader to know from her heart what she experienced as lessons and what the Lord did for her personally while going through the valley for more than five years. She (we) are still in the learning process and will continue until we hear those words from our Lord...
"Well done, good and faithful servants!"*

Trust is a small but very powerful word. It's a word that has taken on new meaning for me throughout this cancer journey. As I lay in an outpatient hospital bed and was told for the very first time that I had colon cancer staring me in the face, I knew I had no other choice but to trust God fully. Proverbs 3:5-6 says, "Trust in the Lord with all your heart and lean not on your own understanding; in all your ways submit to him, and he will make your paths straight." I knew I had to trust God fully with *all* my heart, for I knew God was not surprised by my new diagnosis. He was very aware of the situation I was in. He was not wondering, "What am I going to do with Robin?"

I had to believe in my heart that even in this, God had a plan, and in it, He would receive all the glory.

As my journey continues, there are new decisions to be made and new trails that arise nearly on a daily basis. With each new decision and trial, trusting God takes on new meaning for me. In Matthew 8:23-27, we see Jesus in the boat with his disciples in the middle of a lake. A storm comes out of nowhere and without warning, and the waves sweep over the boat. Jesus was fast asleep. The disciples woke him saying, "Lord save us. We're going to drown." To which the Lord replies, "Oh, ye of little faith, why are you afraid?" Jesus rebuked the winds and waves, and it became calm.

When the storms come in our lives, most of the time it is without warning. Like the disciples in the midst of the storm, we panic. At least in my experience, that is the usual reaction to most of those storms we encounter. Panic brings about more stress in our lives that only Jesus can speak to and bring calm in the midst of the storm.

During the past five-plus years and throughout our physical journeys, the Lord has taught us some very special lessons along the way. Many of us get a measure of these specific lessons, but I'd like to think the Lord has given us an extra measure of these lessons during the storm.

The first of the lessons that stands out to me that has been given in abundant measure and is at the top of my list is peace. Jesus said in John 14:27, "Peace I leave with you; my peace I give you. I do not give to as the world gives. Do not let your hearts be troubled and do not be afraid."

When I received my first cancer diagnosis, I lie on a hospital bed under the effects of anesthesia. I heard those words come from the doctor's mouth, and I began to process them in my mind. I felt as if my heart stopped for a moment. The only reaction I could muster was to lie with tears quietly streaming down my face. I didn't have much to say. Richard asked all the questions as my world was seemingly rocked by my new diagnosis. I remember thinking to myself, "God, I know you are here, and you didn't bring us to Colorado to leave here in only four months." I still knew in my heart that God's hand was in this. I continued to quietly tell him, "God, you're not surprised by this news, for you have a plan. I know you do."

I must tell the truth here: That day was a very difficult day, and a very big "pill to swallow," if you will, and is a moment I will never forget.

Sleep did not come easy that night, if at all. But I remember waking up and trembling in fear. I remember laying there praying, "Lord, I need peace from you." And He came in those moments and gave sweet peace like I had never known before.

You may ask, "How do you receive this kind of peace?" The answer seems so trite and common, but simply put: Spend more time with God in increasing measure. Seek Him. Press in to Him. John 14:27 says again, "Peace I leave with you; my peace I give you. I do not give to you as the world gives. Do not let your hearts be troubled and do not be afraid."

Peace in the Lord is an important factor in living for the Lord in a world so full of fear. I now live in that peace with

Him. People sometimes ask me, "How do you do it? You seem so calm in your journey and all you are going through." To which I respond, "We still have our moments, but our journey is like a hurricane swirling out of control. My world is seemingly swirling out of control and so is our world, but the calm or peace in the midst of that storm lies at the very center. I feel as if the Lord is at the center of the storm and holding us there with all of the tenderness and mercy He can give. We need to know He's in control and just trust Him to bring peace.

Trust is the second lesson we've learned during this journey. Proverbs 3:5-6 is one of my favorite scripture passages and says, "Trust in the Lord with all your heart and lean not on your own understanding. In all your ways acknowledge him, and he will make your paths straight." Wow. Trust him with *all* my heart and acknowledge him in *all* my ways? This requires me to embrace the thought and act that He has it *all* in control. I need to allow him to be in charge and step out of the way. This is not easy and is perhaps the biggest lesson to learn.

During their journey and in the midst of the storm, the disciples needed to trust Jesus and know that he had it all under control. I'm certain most of us, given the same situation, may have reacted much the same way. We can't pretend to trust Him fully when life brings extremely difficult situations. We get fearful, and if we're completely honest, we may even wonder where Jesus is when we're in that "water coming in the boat" experience, but we need to trust Him. Trust Him in the midst of the storm. We need to know in our hearts that He has it *all* under control and let Him control the situation. He will direct us and help us know the way we should go. I try to remember and discipline myself to trust him on a daily basis. It's especially important for me to remember and practice this while I'm lying in bed for two and a half weeks with a fever, and I'm not getting better. I remember praying out loud to God the night before I was admitted to the hospital in January 2013.

"Please Lord, show us what to do. Please take this fever from my body."

I'm thankful for the Lord giving Richard the wisdom to call the doctor's office and prompting them to see me and take action, or I may not have survived. It was discovered only after I was admitted to the hospital that I had a blood infection, which was threatening my life. God heard my cry for help and so many others to which we are so very grateful; we trust Him with *all* our hearts, for I have come to realize God loves those who call out to Him and need Him most. He comes to those who call out to him, who rely on Him, and depend on him while trusting Him with everything. It's where He wants us to be. He desires to meet our needs and desires for us to fully trust Him.

I believe there is purpose in our pain. God's purpose is greater than our pain, and He has a greater purpose than our problems. Our problems and situations are not going to slow down the purpose of God. He will never leave us nor forsake us. This brings me to the next lesson the Lord is actively teaching us, which is *Live by Faith*. To fully rely on God for tomorrow and not worry about tomorrow requires a walk of faith. This walk can only be embraced and lived out one step at a time leaning on Him as we go. Our physical journeys have been just that: a profound reliance on Jesus every step of the way. No, we're not "super Christians" in this walk of dependence and faith. It's just taken these physical trials and our out-of-control situations to depend on Him. We need to learn and know there is nothing impossible with God. And it sometimes takes an out-of-our-control situation, where only God can be the answer for us to learn to depend on him fully.

As I awaken to each new day now, some of my first thoughts of the day and prayers roll off my tongue:

"May I be a blessing to someone today. Lord, May I be in your perfect plan today." When I am admitted to the hospital, I would pray, "Lord, who is it I need to share Jesus with? I'm ready, and I will."

To God be all the glory. It is my desire to be obedient and not worry so much about my physical problems. I want to do my part in serving Jesus and be a blessing to others. Philippians 4:13 says, "I can do all things through Christ who gives me strength."

Dear friend, don't allow worry, fear, and doubt to overtake you and bring you to a place where that "thing" in your life diminishes and clouds your dependence on the Lord. Remain focused on Him no matter what trials come your way. Allow the Spirit of God to breathe a fresh and bold approach to your situation, and He will bring peace in the midst of the storm.

CHAPTER 16

WHEN HEALTH FAILS
IN MARRIAGE

At this juncture, I am compelled to write and interject a very important principle in this story of physical, emotional, financial, and spiritual battles we faced head-on through the valley we were destined to walk together as husband and wife. So many people have asked us, "How do you do it?" What they are asking is, "How do you continue on when you're both dealing with two different stage IV cancers?" I must admit, the journey has been long and arduous. There have been many tears, struggles, fears, disappointments, and every emotion God has instilled within a human being. We've had to deal with them while trying to maintain a somewhat "normalcy" in our marriage and our lives in general. It's been nearly as difficult for our children and families, as they have been on this journey with us since the beginning. These things have a taken a toll on all of us, but we all have one common denominator which is the key to our strength and stability in times like these.

When Robin and I stood before God and witnesses in 1982, we pledged to remain faithful "In sickness and in health." That was the first step in commitment we covenanted before God and man. We knew that at some point, the physical beauty would begin to give way to gravity, and perhaps even sickness which would try our commitment to the core. Along the way, we have had our trials with other sicknesses and an accident which would try our commitment, but we could not imagine the toll dual cancer diagnoses could bring to a marriage relationship. It's a fact that the hardships that come with cancer can and often do erode the core of marriage relationships to the point of separation and divorce, sadly. So what can we attribute our strength, ongoing love, and commitment to while continuing on with poor prognoses glaring at us?

First, let's look to answers found within the pages of Scripture. I know that seems a bit too simplistic for some and perhaps even a bit trite. There has to be more. But there is not more. In fact, without His Word, we would have failed miserably a long time ago. It has brought us courage and strength at times when all else failed. The Bible is alive, and we find great comfort and strength from the scriptures when our strength is all but gone. Robin and I have claimed select scriptures to draw upon in the midst of our trials. Robin's favorite passage is Psalm 118:17, NIV:

"I will not die but live, and will proclaim what the LORD has done."

This passage brings her hope in the midst of uncertain days, and she feels the Lord gave her this scripture in the early days of her diagnosis. She quotes this and treasures this all-important scripture. It's life-giving to her and me.

My favorite scripture is Psalm 46:1-3 NIV:

"God is our refuge and strength, an ever-present help in trouble. Therefore we will not fear, though the earth give way and the mountains fall into the heart of the sea, though its waters roar and foam and the mountains quake with their surging."

I am reminded of His omniscience and power to overcome any obstacle in any situation we go through, even if the world falls apart. In the midst of it all, He will help me.

Second, I would have to attribute our commitment to each other as we are committed to Christ. We are Christ's followers, and Christ's followers don't stop running the race because we find an obstacle in the road. Life has a way of bringing many obstacles along the way. We are only as good to each other as our relationship to Jesus Christ. Our relationship with the Lord is strong. We pray for each other, love each other, care for each other unselfishly and rely on His grace on a daily basis to take us another day—no matter what may come. We could not physically or emotionally maintain our relationship without the relationship we have with our Lord. Someone once said, "Marriage takes three, with Christ at the center of the marriage." We have found this to be undeniably true. Without Him, we would fail. Physically healthy marriages are failing in alarming numbers today, and it's much worse in cases such as ours where one or both partners are in ill health. The strain and stress can be overwhelming at times to the point of utter despair. Without Christ to draw from in our relationship, we would fail.

Third, serve one another and others unselfishly. I've already alluded to this important issue, but when cancer or any other illness comes to a family, it's so easy to become self-centered and focused on your own situation. That's not Christ like at all. My greatest joy is to serve Robin when she's not feeling well. I enjoy making her meals and caring for her. I get satisfaction from knowing I've somehow lifted her burden for the moment and loved her, even if I don't "feel" like it. And she does the same for me. We don't serve each other out of expectation. We serve because Jesus served us, and in turn we can serve each other out of a heart of love and appreciation. The absolute best way to combat depression, in my estimation, is to serve others outside you. Serve your spouse, your family, and go do something for the kingdom of God; you'll find great satisfaction in your life in spite of how you feel. We were not created to be self-serving. God created us serve Him and others around us, and until we begin to put this principle into action, we'll never be completely fulfilled.

The following is my blog entry from www.johnsonsjourney.com entitled, "Love Compels Me to Serve" on January 30, 2013:

"Husbands, love your wives, just as Christ loved the church and gave himself up for her" (Eph. 5:25, NIV)

It's 2:00 a.m. and sleep is not my friend as Robin lies sleeping (hopefully) in a hospital bed this morning. My mind and heart are not willing to turn off the thoughts that so permeate my being in these early morning hours. I slept for a few hours, but now, due to Robin's feverish and two-week-long battle with whatever it is ravaging her body, she was admitted to the hospital to see if they could find out what is causing the fevers that randomly come and go without warning. They are doing a number of blood cultures and tests to help make a determination.

I spoke with our oncologist last night before leaving the hospital, and he said they would do all they could to find out what is causing her the fevers. It may just be from the cancer. He said he has some cancer patients who fight persistent fevers. I know this to be true, as my mother fought persistent high fevers with her liver cancer some years ago, and Robin's is somewhat reminiscent of those days gone by. This is most difficult for me to see Robin go through this, as my mother's battle was very similar.

The past two weeks (perhaps five years) have been a stark reminder to me as to what it truly means to serve my wife just as "Christ loved the church." Love compelled Jesus to serve us, and He gave himself unselfishly for us as the Church. The Bridegroom loves His Bride with a compelling and eternal love that cannot be expressed in any language. It's a love that goes deeper than human comprehension. Paul exhorts husbands to exhibit this kind of love to our wives even if it costs us all we have, including our lives. I enjoy serving my Robin, and I do it with joy. It seems the longer we're married, the more I enjoy serving her.

Two nights ago, I was awakened to the sound of her shivering so severely I thought she was having convulsions. A fever was beginning to take up residence in her. It was my pleasure to serve her the medicine that would help to alleviate the symptoms in about twenty minutes or so. It has been my pleasure to make her meals and watch over her, as she in turn has done so many times for me in the last 30-plus years. I'm not bragging. I'm simply stating, the love that Christ exemplified compels me to serve with a heart that does not keep records of wrongs but only seeks to serve with compassion. I miss her, even though I know she *is only a few miles away. She is not here, but I know she is getting the care she needs to be able to come back to me, which makes her absence more tolerable. We have served each other in these past five years on our cancer journey, and I wouldn't trade a minute of it for all the gold in Fort Knox. Countless hours and days in and out of waiting rooms, tests, and doctor appointments with hundreds of hours driving to and from doctor visits and hospital visits. We've wept, laughed and shared our deepest most intimate thoughts concerning our futures and desires should one or both us go home before the other. These are those things in life we stand at an altar and commit to when we say, "I do." All of the good, bad and ugly that life can bring is here, and we couldn't possibly predict it when we married.*

The real question is, "What are you going to do when life does bring all of those things to your door?" Are you going to lovingly, humbly and unselfishly grasp the opportunity to serve your spouse as "Christ loved the church and gave himself up for her," or will you grumble, complain and look elsewhere for your own selfish desires to be met? Far too many have sought the latter option in hopes of a better outcome, only to find it isn't any better at all; in fact, it can be worse in many cases.

Robin and I have made mistakes and have not had a perfect marriage as some would consider perfect, but we have determined that through trials the most beautiful lessons can be learned by serving each other in the most difficult situations. I know one thing for certain: It is a pleasure serving my lady, and hopefully God will continue to allow me to serve her in the coming days and months. Life without her is not something I want to contemplate.

I saw my renal cell oncologist on Monday and took him copies of all of my scan CD's to view and make recommendations. The radiologist will look at the scans to see if there is anything that could be seen from their perspective to perhaps give some cause for the pain I've had in my side for the past two years. We also talked about this new tumor in my colon and what it means in terms of mortality. He said it could be dealt with surgically and we may have to, as it will begin to cause me problems. He said the nodules in my lungs were small and should not be worrisome in the immediate future, but the colon metastasis changes the outcome short term if I don't do something with it. He wanted me to consider treatment options again and I was not in favor of that, as I know from experience that the side effects can be debilitating. We talked about Robin's diagnosis and struggles, and, simply said, we made a decision to forgo any treatments. We chose quality versus quantity. He understood and respected our decision. For the moment, I am happy to have enough strength and energy to serve Robin, and it's even somewhat of a reprieve to be able to lie down together in the afternoon and nap when we run out of energy.

Robin and I want to thank you all for continuing on this journey with us. Some of you have been following our journey for several years now, and we can't thank you enough for your continued support, love and prayers during the good times and not so good days. Please continue to pray, especially for Robin now, as we enter a new phase in this cancer battle.

Finally, don't take your spouse for granted today, but lovingly and graciously serve one another, for tomorrow it could all change in an instant. We only have this moment to make a meaningful impression

in the lives of those around us and are closest to us. Don't wait until
tomorrow to start.

Serving With Gladness,
Rich and Robin

Fourth, physical attraction is short lived. Intimacy in a marriage is far more than a sexual union. Age and physical illness will begin to take its toll at some point in our lives, and for Robin and I, this happened much quicker than we had anticipated with our cancer diagnoses. If we base our relationship on physical attractiveness and beauty, we will be sorely disappointed as we grow older when sickness enters the scene. Robin and I are more intimate today in our relationship than many couples I know, and it's not based on the physical. We are very aware of the needs of a couple to enjoy the blessing of the marriage bed, but what happens when one or both are stricken with illness? The Lord has helped us to grow in an intimate and secure way emotionally and spiritually, and we are grateful for the relationship we do have. A kiss means more than it ever did. Handholding and caressing are meaningful expressions of our love. I believe the Holy Spirit has made provision in our lives because of our physical limitations. He has developed a greater love and intimacy in us than I never thought possible. All things are possible with God, if we trust Him.

Fifth: take nothing for granted, expect nothing, and appreciate everything.

Robin and I have come to realize the goodness of God in our lives while on this physical journey in a way that has caused us to be so appreciative of everything good that comes our way. We appreciate each other and don't get caught up in trivial, little skirmishes that can become big battles. Our perspectives about those things have changed dramatically through this journey, and complaining will get us nothing but more heartache. It's much easier to find things to complain about—especially when you don't feel well—but it does no one any good to complain about things that just don't matter. It causes people around us to shy away and not want anything to do with the God we say is so good to us. I've always said, "It's a sin to complain." We've been blessed by so many good gifts from people and churches that I can hardly contain myself as I write about it. It has been truly humbling. We feel we don't deserve the goodness we've received in so many expressions of love and support. We take nothing for granted on this journey but look at each new day as a gift. We expect nothing in return, but feel blessed to be able to share our lives and our Lord with others that they may be blessed. And we appreciate every good gift from above. The last few years have been such a blessing to us, as we've been able to travel to places we never would have otherwise. People have been so very gracious to us in supplying us with opportunities to go places and spend quality time together. It's made the journey more tolerable. We could never begin to repay the goodness we've received.

Finally, pray for one another. So many married couples go through their everyday journey in life without ever stopping to take the time to consider their spouse in prayer until something tragic happens. Sadly, if we wait until something tragic happens to pray for our spouse, we miss out on a great opportunity to see God do extraordinary things in their life and in your relationship. It has been a great pleasure to pray for Robin and vice versa the past thirty-one years, but the intensity of my prayers has increased tremendously in these days of physical trial. I can only tell you from experience that if you never get in the habit of praying for your spouse when all is well, you'll be a stranger to praying for them when you need to. Don't be shy about calling out their name before almighty God. Let them know you are praying for their job, health, and everything that concerns them. Don't be afraid and timid about anointing them with oil when they're sick and pray for their healing. I have made it a practice with our children when they were growing up, and I've done it now with Robin as she lays ill. She also prays for me and calls out my name before our Lord. We love each other and care enough to bring each other before our Creator. Uninhibited prayer in the heart of a family will bind that family together in ways that will help to maintain strength and intimacy within the confines of that family.

By no means is this an exhaustive list of the many lessons we've learned in our dual cancer battles in marriage, but by God's grace, we've been able to focus on those things that truly matter for eternity. The focus is not us, but on the Lord who helps us on a daily basis and gives us strength from day to day.

When health fails in any marriage, it becomes tested and tried. It will grow stronger or it will fail. The one common denominator in strong marriages is Jesus Christ and Him alone. Money will fail, physical attraction will fail, and medicine will fail. All will fail except our relationship with Christ and each other. Our relationship is stronger today than it ever was, and it's because we have purposed to remain in Him and commit to staying true to one another no matter what comes our way in this physical valley.

The journey has been long, and it's not over just yet. Jesus Christ has held our hands every step of the way through this valley. No matter what happens, we are confident He is with us "Through The Valley," and He will lead us home.

We will have written this book about our cancer journeys in vain if we didn't give you, the reader, the opportunity to personally know this same Jesus that helps us in our struggles with physical trials. He can and will help you, and He'll give you peace in the midst of your valley if you only put your trust and hope in Him. Ask Him to come into your heart, forgive your sin, and live in you. He's promised to be with you always. He never said life would be easy, but serving Him certainly makes walking through the valley with Him worth every step of the way.

If you have invited Jesus to live in your heart, we would certainly love to hear about it and rejoice with you. Please take the time to drop us a note and tell us. We would also be privileged to pray for your needs. You can write to us at:

Johnson Ministries
1203 E. Fieldstone Dr.
Ozark, MO 65721

Email: richlee137@gmail.com
Web site: www.johnsonsjourney.com